LEARNING DISABILITIES IN THE PRIMARY CLASSROOM

LEONORA HARDING

CROOM HELM
London • Sydney • Wolfeboro, New Hampshire

© 1986 Leonora Harding
Croom Helm Ltd, Provident House, Burrell Row,
Beckenham, Kent, BR3 1AT

Croom Helm Australia Pty Ltd, Suite 4, 6th Floor,
64-76 Kippax Street, Surry Hills, NSW 2010, Australia

British Library Cataloguing in Publication Data

Harding, Leonora
     Learning disabilities in the primary
     classroom.
     1. Learning disabilities 2. Education,
     Elementary
     I. Title
     371.9′043   LC4704

     ISBN 0-7099-3785-7
     ISBN 0-7099-4764-X Pbk

Croom Helm, 27 South Main Street,
Wolfeboro, New Hampshire 03894-2069, USA

Library of Congress Cataloging-in-Publication Data

Harding, Leonora, 1944-
     Learning disabilities in the primary classroom

     1. Learning disabled children — Education — Great
Britain. I. Title.
LC4706.G7H37 1986   371.9   86-24005
ISBN 0-7099-3785-7
ISBN 0-7099-4764-X (Pbk.)

**Printed and bound in Great Britain
by Billing & Sons Limited, Worcester.**

CONTENTS

ACKNOWLEDGEMENTS

Permission by the following sources for reproduction of illustrations is gratefully acknowledged.

Figure 6.2: From: <u>Principles of Instructional Design</u> by Robert M. Gagné and Leslie J. Briggs. Copyright © 1974 by Holt, Rinehart and Winston, Inc. Reprinted by permission of CBS College Publishing.

Figure 6.3: From: <u>The Psychology of Mathematics for Instruction</u> by L. B. Resnick and W. W. Ford. Copyright © 1981 by Laurence Erlbaum, Inc. Reprinted by permission of CBS College Publishing.

1. LEARNING-DISABLED CHILDREN AND THEIR EDUCATION

WHO ARE LEARNING-DISABLED CHILDREN?

Terry is a well-built robust child of eight years. The middle child of a family of three, his main problem is in reading. This seems all the more pronounced as his younger sister, aged six years, is a fluent reader. On the surface, he is a happy-go-lucky child, liking to play outside, climbing and playing football. However, this physical activity may mask a number of problems. He is poorly co-ordinated, and other children do not like playing with him. At school his class teacher describes him as a 'jittery youngster' who finds it difficult to sit still. He has had speech therapy from the age of four and still has difficulty in pronouncing words, though he told the story of 'Glack and the Beanstalk' with great vigour.

Terry's academic progress is very slow. He has a reading age of five years and eleven months on the Schonell test, and he writes poorly. His ability in arithmetic is a little better and he seems to be keeping up with the rest of the class. When tested with the Wechsler Intelligence Scale for Children he obtained a Verbal IQ of 121 and a Performance IQ of 86. Visual-motor abilities seemed to be poor as his drawings from copy on the Bender-Gestalt test were inaccurate.

This is only a brief description of a child with learning difficulties. It is fairly superficial in its description of the child's character and mentions a few significant test results. However, although this description is incomplete, it serves to illustrate the individuality and complexity of each learning disabled child.

We can say that we have some information about what the child appears to be like, from observation, from reports of the school teacher and from his or her parents. This information may give us some insight into the personal misery the child is likely to be experiencing. In this case, Terry's high achieving younger sister, his need for activity both inside and outside school, and so on. It also gives some insight into personal strengths. Here the child's love of stories was apparent despite his speech problems.

Test information can also give some indication of

strengths and weaknesses, and may serve as a pointer towards further information gathering. In the case of Terry, it seems that all his strengths are verbal ones (despite his speech difficulty) and his weaknesses are in the perceptual motor area. So we can set up a working hypothesis which gives us an indication of which areas to search next. In the case of Terry we might want to see whether he attempts to use his strength when learning to read or in other tasks. We might expect him to use linguistic cues in reading and that perceptual-motor difficulties would be obvious here also. The importance of setting up such working hypotheses cannot be overemphasised.

Each learning-disabled child (indeed every child) is a person with individual strengths and weaknesses. It is only through the exploration of the strengths and weaknesses that a proper remedial program can be devised, one which helps the child to learn through his strengths, whilst building up or compensating for his weaknesses. This book attempts to delineate the various strengths and weaknesses experienced by learning disabled children and some specific methods of remediation. The desirability of such diagnostic formulation and remediation has been apparent since the 1981 Education Act, which followed on the Warnock Report of 1978 and was an important milestone in our understanding and treatment of learning disabled children.

The Warnock Report and its Aftermath

The Warnock Report (1978) was revolutionary in its recommendation that the categorisation of handicapped children be abolished. Such categorisation had been prevalent for many years and was a feature of the 1944 Education Act. In all, eleven categories of children were in common usage, ranging from maladjustment to the partially deaf and educationally subnormal. This categorisation was in part responsible for the segregation of handicapped children into special schools. Warnock recommended that the term 'children with special needs' replace the existing categorisation. This was in order to emphasise the needs of children rather than their handicap. Thus Warnock was providing a more appropriate educational rather than a medical perspective.

The Warnock Report also recommended that the term 'children with learning disabilities' should be used as a term to cover those children who are categorised as ESN and those with educational difficulties who are presently covered by the remedial services. Such learning disability could be deemed severe, moderate or mild. Children of average or above average intelligence who had a learning problem might be called 'children with a specific learning disability' if so desired.

The reasoning behind the abolition of categorisation was partly the desire to treat all children as individuals with individual needs, but also because categorisation was seen as logistically impossible since most learning-disabled children have more than one learning disability. Therefore many children would present problems because they would fall into two or more categories simultaneously. A severely mentally-handicapped child, for example, usually has an additional physical handicap and may be blind or deaf. At the other end of the scale a child who has problems with reading may have additional speech and auditory discrimination problems. A clumsy child or a hyperactive child would be likely to have perceptual problems and difficulty with the three Rs.

In the 1944 Education Act it was deemed necessary to educate each child according to 'age, ability and aptitude'. The 1981 Act revised this by adding the words '...and to any special educational needs he may have'. A child was said to have special educational needs if 'he has a learning difficulty which calls for special educational provision to be made for him'. Learning difficulties are of three kinds, as outlined in this act. Firstly, where the child has greater difficulties in learning 'than the majority of children of his age'. Secondly, where he has a disability or handicap 'which prevents or hinders him from making use of the educational provision'. Finally, there are the children under five years of age who would fall into the previous two categories whenever they do reach the appropriate age.

This Education Act has been criticised as presenting a circular definition (Wedell, Welton and Vorhaus, 1982) and as being rather less precise than the Warnock recommendations (Brennan, 1982). The Warnock Report specifies that the provision be in terms of equipment and resources including new buildings, the provision of a special education curriculum and 'the social and emotional climate in which education takes place'. The provision of the special education curriculum might seem an especially tall order and this is one reason why the Warnock Report emphasises teacher training. Certainly the employment of teachers and other professionals with appropriate background and training would be necessary to implement such a recommendation.

The 1981 Education Act has also had important

sequelae (see Newell, 1983). One important feature of it was that each child in need of special education had to have a statement made of his or her educational needs. In addition to describing the child's specific needs, this statement has sections which attempt to outline how these needs shall be met in terms of school arrangements and educational provision. There are important appendices which give information from parents, teachers and several professional advisers. All those who are called on to give such information are advised that their information be given in three categories which are:

1. Description of the child's functioning
    a) Description of the child's strengths
       and weaknesses.
    b) Factors in the child's environment.
    c) Relevant aspects of the child's history.

2. Aims of provision
    a) General areas for development.
    b) Specific areas of weakness or gaps in skills
       acquisition which impede the child's progress.
    c) Suggested methods and approaches.

3. Facilities and resources

        Thus the information needed for each child is quite precise. Any professionals who are involved with children in need of special education will have to have a clear idea of the learning difficulties experienced by the child and how these might be remedied.
        There are other important developments in Special Education which have arisen because of the Warnock Report and the 1981 Act. Not the least of these is the policy of integration of children with special needs into ordinary schools (see Hegarty, Pocklington and Lucas, 1981).

The Incidence of Learning Disability

The estimate of children in need of special education lies somewhere between 15 and 20%. This former figure is in agreement with the 1944 Education Act (14 to 17%). Pringle et al, (1966) gave a figure of between 13% and 15% of seven-year-olds. The 13% is the figure given by headteachers as an estimate of the number of children who could, with some advantage, have been given special educational help in ordinary schools. In a follow-up study of all the children in the study at age sixteen years, 13% were receiving help in ordinary schools, 1.9%

were in special schools and 3% were estimated as being in need of special education. Special help within schools was deemed necessary for a further 5.5% (Fogelman, 1976). Hence, this is a total of 23.4% in need of special education. Rutter, Tizard and Whitmore's (1970) Isle of Wight survey judged that for four types of handicap (intellectual, educational, psychiatric disorder and physical handicap) 16.1% of children in the nine to eleven age group had a chronic or recurrent handicap. This figure of one in six children is seen as an underestimate in view of the fact that not all handicaps were covered. Most of these figures would be in support of the statement given by the Warnock Report that 'one in six children at any one time and one in five children at some time in their school career will be in need of special education'.

A distinction is often made between the total group (the 20%) and the larger fraction (the 18%) who represent the children seen in ordinary schools. The 18% does not usually appear in estimates of children receiving special education (see Table 1.1) given as a total of 152,326 children. This represents 1.49% of the total school population of England (Special Education Forward Trends, 1982). 1.41% of children were in special schools and is the number of children who had been ascertained as in need of special education. It is with this 18% that this book is directly concerned. It represents the five or six children with special educational needs in every class of thirty children.

Table 1.1: Numbers of Children Receiving Special Education by Category, in England and Wales

Category	1977	1979	1982
Blind	1,255	1,168	1,155
Partially sighted	2,205	2,819	2,774
Deaf	3,627	4,115	3,750
Partially hearing	2,111	7,256	7,023
Physically handicapped	13,083	16,677	15,148
Delicate	4,404	6,893	4,951
Maladjusted	13,687	22,402	16,047
ESN Mod	55,698)		65,604
Sev	22,839)	119,005	27,597
Epileptic	2,096	1,689	2,522
Speech defect	4,715	2,972	4,828
Autistic	562		927
In hosp schools	8,979		
Total	135,261	184,996	152,326

Sources: Brennan, 1982
         Special Education Forward Trends, 1982
         Statistics of Education, 1977, 1979.

Nevertheless, there are some important pieces of information to be gleaned from the statistics in special education (see Table 1.1). The 1982 figures show some important trends when compared with previous years (see also Brennan, 1982). Firstly, there is some fluctuation in the numbers of children in certain categories, that is, in the deaf and partially hearing, children with speech defects and delicate children. Secondly, there seems to be a slight increase in the numbers of maladjusted and autistic children. There is also an increase in the numbers of children in ordinary schools over time. The majority of partially hearing and over a fifth of the children ascertained as being ESN (M), delicate, epileptic, speech defective and physically handicapped are now educated in ordinary schools (see Table 1.2).

Table 1.2: Distribution of Children Receiving Special Education in England and Wales in 1982

Category	Maintained and non-maintained special schools	Maintained primary and secondary schools		Total
		Special classes	Ordinary classes	
Blind	1,080	21	54	1,155
Partially sighted	1,731	149	894	2,774
Deaf	2,867	481	402	3,750
Partially hearing	1,342	2,544	3,137	7,023
Physically handicapped	11,488	529	3,131	15,148
Delicate	3,391	257	1,303	4,951
Maladjusted	13,177	1,382	1,488	16,047
ESN Mod.	55,561	7,644	2,399	65,604
Ser.	27,252	235	110	27,597
Epileptic	1,530	64	928	2,522
Speech defect	2,252	1,078	1,498	4,828
Autistic	679	118	130	927
Totals	122,350	14,502	15,474	152,326

Source: Special Education Forward Trends, 1982.

Hence we can expect that many children with ascertained handicaps will be in ordinary schools in addition to the 18% without obvious handicap who are still in need of special education.

A further point which Rutter et al (1970) emphasised is that many of these children will have more than one learning disability. Of the quite severely handicapped children he surveyed, one quarter of the children had more than one handicap. For example, of the educationally handicapped (children with attainments well below average) 43% had additional handicaps. This category would be those children usually labelled remedial who are found in ordinary schools. It would seem likely then that two or three of the five or six children in the class of thirty who have special educational needs would have more than one learning difficulty.

LEARNING-DISABLED CHILDREN IN THE NORMAL CLASSROOM

Apart from the physically handicapped or partially hearing child whose handicap is obvious and who gains sympathetic attention, there is a small group of learning-disabled children in every class. They are often euphemistically referred to as slow learners or remedial, and sometimes less kindly by children as dumbos, thickies or worse. Unfortunately these attitudes may be unwittingly perpetuated by the teacher, who is constantly frustrated by the lack of progress in this group despite frequent attention. The children may go to the remedial teacher for half an hour a day, but this is a drop in the ocean of time that the class teacher has to teach them. It is hardly surprising then that the class teacher comes out with such remarks to the visiting psychologist as 'Oh, you can see those children any time you like, I can't do anything with them.'

The Warnock Report directly addresses the needs of children in so-called remedial groups, who 'have a wide variety of individual needs, sometimes linked to psychological or physical factors, which call for skilled and discriminating attention by staff in assessment, the devising of suitable programs and the organisation of group or individual teaching whether in ordinary or special classes'. Here we are given some idea of the complexity of the problem of educating children with learning difficulties in the ordinary school. The children have widely differing needs, some in terms of physical or other handicap, some with emotional problems and most with learning difficulties in more than one area. In order that these children can attain according to their ability, they need highly skilled and personal teaching. There is a great need for children's learning difficulties to be individually assessed and provided for in terms of individual programs. This is a mammoth task for the ordinary school teacher, but not an insurmountable one, as I hope to demonstrate in this book.

The Prepared Classroom

How do we cater for such children in the normal school day in the normal school environment? There are two main approaches to this problem, that is by remedial withdrawal group and by special class. The remedial withdrawal group is a group which is taken out of the ordinary classroom from time to time to be given remedial teaching, and seems to be the most popular arrangement at this time, especially if the remedial teacher works in the normal classroom from time to time. It is seen as the better alternative, largely because the children are mainly integrated into the normal classroom, and also a large number of children can be catered for in the school day. In the special class children will get more suitable work and attention to their specific needs, but they may be seen as different from other children, which it is argued is a stigma that should be avoided if at all possible. Of course children who are part of a withdrawal group may also be stigmatised in this way.

How can the classroom or remedial teacher organise her classroom to the benefit of the children with learning difficulties and the ordinary children? Whether the classroom is a special class or an ordinary class, one approach is to think of the classroom as a prepared environment, in the sense used by Maria Montessori (1945), as a learning environment which caters for the individual needs of all children. In such an environment children can work at their own level, with the aid of the teacher. The setting up of such an environment has been widely adopted in the infant school following the recommendations of the Plowden Report (1967). There is no reason why such ideas should not be adopted in the junior and even secondary school and is indeed recommended by some. Such an environment needs a great deal of preparation on the part of the teacher, but, if properly executed, individual pupils will benefit. I have seen such methods adopted both by an ordinary primary school class and a special class.

The special class situation which demonstrates a

prepared environment is one catering for a group of twenty-five children aged 7 to 11 years. It was developed by a newly trained teacher for the then New University of Ulster in Northern Ireland, and is depicted in Figure 1.1. The classroom has a conventional arrangement of tables and chairs, with the addition of a grouping of six where the teacher can sit with a small group of pupils who are the focus of attention at any particular time. Around the walls of the classroom are arranged a series of bays with a range of activities related to the children's abilities. The areas in this particular classroom were, a Number area, a Reading corner, English corner with word and letter games and a Construction area. In this particular classroom there were no creative play materials though it might be considered an important adjunct. This is because this particular teacher thinks it is important to emphasise work and to develop confidence in the children by demonstrating to them their success in the three Rs. In addition the teacher has set up two double-sided activity boards, which children complete during the day. On the Mathematics activity board there is on one side a set of squares to be coloured in, each with a number. When the squares are coloured in correctly (in answer to some questions) they form a picture. Each child has to do a small amount and when the page is complete the page may be taken off to reveal another puzzle underneath. On the English activity board there are the initial lines of two limericks. The children have to make up alternative endings. Each child in the class knows that in the course of the morning he or she will have to do a Mathematics work card and an English work card (graded at his or her level). In addition, he will read to the teacher and may have a lesson with her either individually or in a group. He or she will usually be set additional tasks at the termination of the group lesson, for example, playing sound lotto or phonic rummy, or following a program on the class computer. Morale in this class is usually high, as the teacher ensures a degree of success for each child and is constantly praising effort. An atmosphere of industry prevails.

How much better is the experience of the learning disabled child in such a class, than that of the child in the ordinary classroom where he is constantly finding he cannot do the work set for the rest of the class. But, such progressive methods have been criticised (Bennett, 1976) because it is claimed that the achievement level of the class as a whole is not so great as in the traditional school system. However, we do not know the

Figure 1.1: Special classroom for children with learning
disabilities

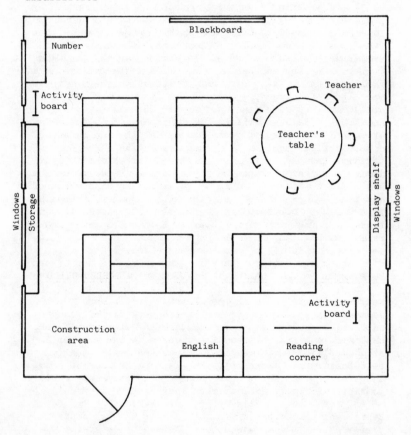

effect of the ability to work independently and creatively by children educated in such methods on their achievements and contribution to society as a whole in adult life. We might claim that a lag of six months in achievement at age eleven is a small price to pay if children are to have a greater ability to achieve their potential in adult life.

One important aspect of the child's experience of a prepared classroom is that it fosters self directed learning. Such learning may be better preparation for life where individual initiative reaps rewards. It is argued by Bruner (1971), Kohl (1970), Piaget and Inhelder (1969) that such self directed activity is important for the development of creative and autonomous people, who are capable 'of new ideas rather than just repeating the old' (Piaget, 1964). The integration of children with special educational needs into the ordinary school can also help to foster self esteem. In a survey of research on integration Hegarty, Pocklington and Lucas (1981) came to the conclusion that there was 'the broad concensus among teachers, parents and pupils themselves that they had benefited in terms of social and emotional development by taking part in an integration program'. This emotional and social development was ascertained in terms of self-confidence, adjustment to handicap and relationships with other children.

PRINCIPLES OF EDUCATION FOR THE LEARNING-DISABLED CHILD

Many researchers, including Frostig and Maslow, (1973), Johnson and Myklebust (1967) and Wedell (1972), have outlined principles for educating learning-disabled children. Many of these principles are the same as for all children, for example, meaningfulness, developing self respect, teaching to the child's level. However, there are some principles which are of prime importance to the learning disabled child.

Behaviourist Principles

Even though behaviourist principles have been largely applied to behaviour problems in children (see, for example, Herbert, 1975, 1981) the principles are relevant to the teaching of learning disabled children. The effects of reinforcement, non-reinforcement and punishment may even be greater in learning-disabled children because of their previous reinforcement histories. Many children have developed a negative attitude to work because they have experienced little reinforcement in their lives. Zigler (1968) showed that many learning-disabled children had developed such a negative reaction tendency that it took some time for them to respond to trusted adults. We may state that the first principle to be applied to learning-disabled children is to reinforce and reinforce again, to develop a pattern of gaining and maintaining success.

Punishment is equally as potent at discouraging the child. An occasional failure may enhance the performance of normal children (Child, 1978) but may be extremely detrimental for the learning disabled child as graphically expressed by Holt (1966). We have all seen the child who repeatedly gets even the simplest sum wrong. Yet it is very difficult for the class teacher to set the learning-disabled child tasks at the right level. This is what Hunt (1961) terms the 'problem of the match' between the task difficulty level and the ability of the child. How often have we heard the aphorism 'start where the child is at' and yet have failed to carry that principle out in practice.

Task Analysis

One important development in special education which can assist in finding where 'the child is at' is that of task analysis or instructional design (Gagné, 1970; Gagné and Briggs, 1974). This quite simply is a procedure whereby a task (say an addition sum of numbers up to 100) is broken down into its prerequisite skills. If a child then is failing in this task we can look at the prerequisite skills to see whether he or she has mastered those. If not, then the prerequisite skills can be taught. With reference to reading, task analysis may sound something akin to the old concept of reading readiness. Reading readiness development was based on the assumption that certain skills were prerequisites for reading, for example, a certain degree of language development, visual discrimination or auditory sequential memory. Whilst simple tests of auditory and visual discrimination were thought to be valuable in determining whether a child is ready to read, Downing and Thackray (1971) point out that most reading readiness tests were too broad and not related to specific reading tasks. Downing and Thackray comment that instead of asking 'Has the child developed reading readiness?', a more reasonable question to ask would be 'When is this particular child ready for this particular reading program?'. Hence, reading readiness tests were not based on the analysis of a particular reading task. In contrast, task analysis, when applied to reading, would be the analysis of a specific reading task for a particular child. For example, we may find that a child is unable to read 'This is Fluff, the cat' but is quite able to read each word when presented in isolation. We can ask what are the prerequisites for this task besides word recognition. A reasonable memory span would also be necessary, as well as the ability to sequence words by scanning visually. Precise task analysis can lead to important remedial procedures when carried out with a particular child or small group in mind.

The Diagnostic-Remedial Method

Another important principle in special education is that of teaching to the strengths whilst remediating the area of weakness. This is referred to as building up the deficits whilst teaching to the integrity by Johnson and Myklebust (1967). A child with a specific reading disability may have no visual perceptual deficits, for example, but may have problems on the auditory side as reflected in poor speech and problems with auditory discrimination and sound blending. Johnson and Myklebust would advocate teaching this child to read using an ideo-visual approach (his strength) whilst at the same time giving training in speech, and auditory discrimination and awareness (his weakness). It is interesting to note that this particular method has been used successfully with Down's Syndrome children in recent years. This principle should be based on the diagnosis of individual strengths and weaknesses in the child, but can also be used with small groups.

The diagnosis of children's specific learning problems and the setting up of remedial methods based on such analysis has been called the diagnostic-remedial process (Bateman, 1966). There are, broadly speaking, five steps in the process which can be arranged diagrammatically in a circular fashion (see Figure 1.2) to demonstrate that the original hypothesis needs revision over time.

Such a diagnostic-remedial procedure is essentially behind the recommendation of the 1981 Education Act that each child in need of special education shall have a statement setting out his or her specific educational needs. This statement is subject to revision on a yearly basis. For the class teacher of remedial children or children for whom no such statement has to be made accurate diagnosis with formal tests is both unwieldy and unnecessary. Simple tests and accurate observations can lead to the teacher setting up a reasonable working hypothesis of the child's problems. Such a hypothesis

Figure 1.2: Diagrammatic representation of the
diagnostic-remedial process (after Bateman, 1966)

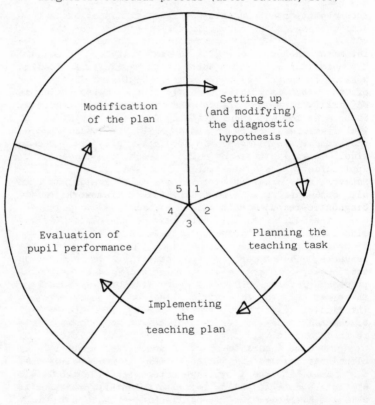

can be modified subsequently when the results of the various remedial procedures used are known.

A Framework for the Diagnostic-Remedial Process

This diagnostic-remedial process is very different from the normal methods of teaching used by the classroom teacher, in that it requires ongoing assessment of each individual child's needs. For the classroom teacher who has little training in special education this might seem like an onerous task. He may or may not have the services of an educational psychologist to call on to assist in this process, but in any case he has no need of such complicated procedures as a psychologist might use. What is needed is a set of specific guidelines for setting up diagnostic hypotheses and making remedial recommendations.

Initially the classroom teacher will be setting up working hypotheses, hunches if you like, about the basis of the child's problems and the teacher needs some kind of framework in which to conceptualise these problems. Such a framework can be given by the conceptual model of the Illinois Test of Psycholinguistic Abilities or ITPA (McCarthy and Kirk, 1961). This is a test which is widely used in the USA but it does not seem entirely applicable to British populations (Clark, 1970). However, it is not the test which I am advocating the use of, but the model of the ITPA adds a framework for the diagnostic-remedial method (see Figure 1.3).

The ITPA is based on the concept of learning disability 'which refers to specific retardation or disorder in one or more of the processes of speech, language, perception, behaviour, reading, spelling, writing or numerature'. It refers to two levels of processing (representational and automatic/sequential), three processes (receptive or decoding, association or integration, and expressive or encoding) and two channels of communication (auditory-vocal and visual-motor). This is not an inclusive list of possible abilities. For example the tactile-motor channel as used by the blind-deaf person (e.g. Helen Keller) is not specified.

What is meant by these categories? The two levels of language organisation refer to voluntary processes of which we are aware (representational) as well as the more automatic well learned skills. For example, describing what happened yesterday (verbal encoding) or writing down sums from the blackboard (visual decoding) would be skills at the representational level. But many things that we do are almost entirely automatic, getting up and getting dressed (visual-motor automatic), constructing·

Figure 1.3: The Clinical Model of the Illinois Test of Psycholinguistic Abilities
(after McCarthy and Kirk, 1961)

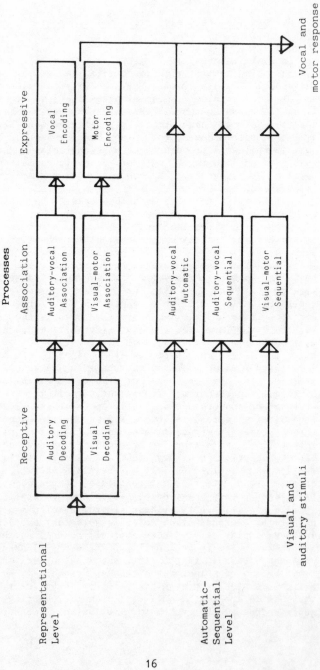

Processes

Receptive — Association — Expressive

Representational
Level

Auditory Decoding → Auditory-vocal Association → Vocal Encoding

Visual Decoding → Visual-motor Association → Motor Encoding

Automatic-
Sequential
Level

Auditory-vocal Automatic

Auditory-vocal Sequential

Visual-motor Sequential

Visual and auditory stimuli

Vocal and motor response

sentences (auditory-verbal automatic) and keeping a telephone number in our head (auditory sequential memory). This is an important distinction as many of the skills children acquire in reading and writing are initially attended to voluntarily and later become automatic.

The division into three levels of processing is important. Teachers are probably aware of the distinction between encoding and decoding as exemplified by the child who understands and carries out all instructions (that is, he understands language well), but speaks very little. Channels of language input and output will be especially obvious when the child with a physical or sensory disability is considered, where one or more of these channels may be nonfunctioning or underfunctioning. Less obviously learning disabled children can however have learning disabilities in one or more channels.

LEARNING DISABILITY AND MINIMAL BRAIN DAMAGE

Early views of learning-disabled children rested on the notion that such children had some brain damage. Strauss and Lehtinen's work of 1947 described several behaviours which were thought to be characteristic of brain-injured children. The main ones are forced responsiveness to stimuli, perseveration and disinhibition. Today a child with these characteristics would be called hyperactive. The neurological basis for such problem behaviour cannot be demonstrated in every case but research would lend support to the idea that there may be some brain dysfunction in many cases (Ross and Ross, 1976).

Minimal brain damage was implicated in other conditions. Most notable, of course, was the syndrome of word blindness (Hinshelwood, 1917) or developmental dyslexia (Orton, 1937). Many people now consider that the term dyslexia is inadvisable (DES Report, 1972) yet a number of specialists in learning disability acknowledge that there may be some minimal brain damage at least in some cases (Farnham-Diggory, 1978; Jorm, 1979; Lerner, 1971). It is self-evident that minimal brain damage cannot be demonstrated for each individual child with a learning disability. It must remain as a working hypothesis. Yet knowledge of brain functioning and brain damage effects in adults can assist in our understanding of learning disabilities, if only because such knowledge helps us to conceptualise the problem.

It is useful to have some working knowledge of neurological development and hemispherical functioning of the child. One aspect of such development which is important is the notion that the young child's brain is relatively plastic. This means that functions need not be laid down in specific areas. The occipital-parietal area of the left hemisphere, for example, usually subserves language in an adult, but if a young child receives some kind of injury to this area then language can become localised in a different area. Another area can take over the localisation of that function. Of course, some functions are not so flexible as language; brain damage to the motor areas will always lead to some spasticity for example. Luria (1973) is really referring to this fact when he refers to his law of diminishing specificity. He sees that certain functions, the sensory ones, are localised in specific areas of the brain. For example, the functions of vision, hearing, touch and movement are localised. Secondary associative functions are localised to a lesser extent. For example, the association of vision with hearing, which would be important in reading, is not so strictly localised though usually the left parietal area subserves this function. Tertiary functions, of which intelligence might be considered the main one, are even more diffusely scattered. These secondary and tertiary functions also develop quite slowly in the child and so a child with slow brain development might be expected to show some developmental delay with regard to these functions.

Luria also maintains that these secondary and tertiary functions are lateralised to different sides of the brain. Usually the left hemisphere develops in relation to speech and language, both receptive and expressive. It also develops all higher forms of thinking concerned with speech, such as active verbal memory, verbal reasoning and logic. Because of this localisation in the left hemisphere is more precise; for example rapid serial processing is carried out in this hemisphere. It is probably not an accident that motor functions which are localised in this hemisphere are fast, detailed and finely coordinated in the activity of the right hand.

By comparison the right hemisphere usually develops holistically, functions being represented more diffusely. So the right hemisphere functions include pictorial and facial perception, some mathematical functioning, art and social perception, music and the perception of environmental stimuli. Motor functions which are represented in the right hemisphere are those of the left side of the body, including the left hand, the steadying hand.

In our description of learning-disabled children,

it is such knowledge of the laterisation of functions which can assist in understanding. This knowledge can help us to understand why certain learning difficulties are often found together (for example, speech and language problems and reading difficulties are often associated). Problems in the area of visual perception are often assocated with mathematical difficulties. These associations are quite tenuous as the skills themselves are quite complex. For example, a child with a reading difficulty might have a language problem or a perceptual-motor difficulty or a difficulty in making visual-verbal associations. However, this book is organised in accordance with the lateralisation of functions. The left hemisphere functions of language, reading and writing are discussed first. The right hemisphere skills of perceptual-motor functioning, mathematics (to an extent) and social perception follow.

This neurological information, though presented in simplified form, has certain implications for the education of learning-disabled children. Our knowledge of the plasticity of the young child's brain and the possibility of retraining would imply that early screening for learning difficulties is desirable. If such plasticity is to be utilised then training programs should be given as early as possible. Indeed, this is stressed by several researchers in the field of special education (for example, Chazan and Laing, 1982).

Secondly, such learning difficulties in adults with brain damage serve as examples and demonstrate how certain learning processes are affected independently of others. In the case of adult dyslexia, for example, there may be two separate types due to damage of different areas of the brain. This can give some indication that there may be different types of reading difficulty shown in children. At least there seem to be visual and language subtypes.

SUMMARY

Learning-disabled children form a widely divergent group of individuals with individual strengths and weaknesses. One in five primary school children are likely to have such a learning disability at some time in their school careers. It is important that the needs of these children are recognised by the ordinary school teacher and dealt with in the normal primary school. I have argued that a remedial classroom is the best place for this, where at least a trained teacher can attempt to recognise the child's strengths and weaknesses and to use such knowledge in remediation.

2. SPEECH AND LANGUAGE DIFFICULTIES

There is a great variety of speech and language
difficulties in primary school children. It may be
difficult for the classroom teacher to ascertain whether
a child's language is just slow to develop or whether his
speech and language is abnormal and pathological. The
slow to develop child will 'grow out of it', but the
child with more serious abnormalities will not.

It is important for the teacher to be aware of the
normal range of children's language in the primary
school. It would be safe to say that children beyond the
age of seven or eight years should not be experiencing
articulation difficulties, though these are fairly common
in five- or six-year-olds. Junior school children should
be capable of talking in sentences, in using all tenses,
negatives and so on. The work of Lenneberg (1967) has
given a definitive outline of this development and
indicates that by the age of four years language is fully
established and after this 'deviations from the adult
norm tend to be more in style than in grammar'.

In recent years there has been an increase in the
number of children seen and treated for speech and
language problems. This is unlikely to be due to the
actual number of children with speech and language
problems being on the increase but because of an
increased awareness of the importance of early
intervention of speech and language problems.

The Quirk Report (1972) concluded that 3% of
children in ordinary schools suffered from speech
disorders though only 2% required a speech therapist.
However, it was thought that nearer 3% of preschool
children required speech therapy, which again emphasises
the need for early intervention. The figures given in
the Quirk Report, which are shown in Table 2.1, give an
estimate for numbers of children requiring speech therapy
though there are other categories of children, for
example, partially hearing and autistic children, who are
not included in these figures. The inclusion of adults
also would increase the figure to well over 300,000
children and adults in need of speech therapy services in
this country. According to the Quirk Report this figure
'can err only in being too low'. When we compare these
figures with those receiving special education (in the

figures given in Chapter 1) one can only observe that these numbers were not being catered for in 1977 especially in ordinary schools. Also, we cannot be sure that the special education which ESN and physically handicapped children are receiving includes speech therapy. There has been a vast increase in speech therapy services following the Quirk Report, but if these figures are anything to go by it is likely that the demand for speech therapists far outstrips the supply.

Table 2.1: Estimates of children requiring and receiving special education in the form of speech therapy (England, Wales and Scotland)

			Numbers requiring speech therapy	Numbers receiving special educ.1977
Children in ord. schools	9 millions	2	180,000	4,700
ESN(M)	60,000	20	12,000	55,000
ESN(S)	35,000	50	17,500	23,000
Physically handicapped	12,000	25	3,000	13,000
Preschool	2 millions	3	60,000	

Sources: Quirk Report (1972)
          Statistics in Education 1977

It is not the intention to cover the excellent work done by speech therapists here, but to give teachers some guidelines as to what constitutes a problem in language or speech, and when a speech therapist should be consulted. Simple methods of ascertaining speech and language problems will be covered though for more sophisticated tests the reader is referred to Muller, Munro and Code (1981). Types of remedial assistance which the teacher may give are also covered. It is often pointed out that the teacher should only give assistance in the case of speech and language problems which are more properly dealt with by a speech therapist or teacher of the deaf. However, in view of the gap between supply and demand for speech therapists already mentioned, a well informed teacher can help to alleviate some of the minor problems.

THE CLASSIFICATION OF SPEECH AND LANGUAGE PROBLEMS

At this point it may be useful to look at the areas of speech and language which may be affected. The distinction is usually made between speech (which involves the production of sounds) and language per se. Language can be further subdivided into grammar or syntax and meaning or semantics, or as a tripartite three level system as given by Garman (1980).

Figure 2.1: Levels of linguistic analysis (after Garman, 1980)

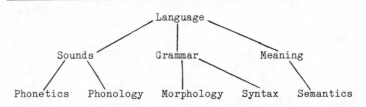

These distinctions may be useful when one wants to describe the different problems that can occur though, as Crystal (1980) points out, the differences are not real since in talking all these aspects of language are combined. The emphasis should perhaps be on a system of communication which is not visual or tactile.

The classification of speech and language problems is usually in accordance with these divisions, though Crystal prefers to include receptive disorders such as deafness, as given in Figure 2.2.

Figure 2.2: Classification of speech and language problems

Pathologies of reception -	Deafness, partial hearing and auditory discrimination
Central pathologies -	Aphasia (expressive and receptive), agnosia, dyspraxia, dysarthria and developmental language disorders
Pathologies of production -	Fluency, voice and articulation.

Such a system, whilst inclusive of all problems, is the domain of the language pathologist. For the teacher the more common problems can be classified in a similar vein and these will be discussed in turn. Emphasis will be placed on those disabilities where a specialist is not always available. For example, profound deafness will not be discussed as it falls outside the domain of the class teacher in the ordinary school. The rest of the chapter will be organised as follows:

Figure 2.3: Proposed classification of children's language difficulties

Receptive difficulties -	a) Deaf and partial hearing
	b) Auditory discrimination
Language difficulties -	Developmental language disorders
Speech problems -	a) Voice
	b) Fluency (stuttering and stammering)
	c) Articulation

DIFFICULTIES IN THE RECEPTION OF LANGUAGE

Difficulties in the reception of language can be divided into rather gross impairment of hearing and at a fine level the discrimination of sounds. These two groups will be considered in turn.

a) The Deaf and Partially Hearing

Deafness is a form of sensory deprivation which may have an effect, not only on speech, but on the development of thinking in the child. The deaf child has profound or total loss of auditory sensitivity, whereas the partially hearing child hears varying amounts of the distinguishing features of speech. What he hears and preceives depends on a combination of several factors, such as the faintness of sound, the distance between the speaker and the listener, noise background and so on. An audiogram registers hearing and hearing loss in terms of loudness which is measured by decibel loss.

The characteristics and education of the deaf and partially hearing child are well covered by such authors as Myklebust (1964) and Conrad (1979). However, it may be useful to discuss a number of issues here which may be relevant to the ordinary school teacher who may have a deaf or partially hearing child in her class for at least some of the school day. The first area is that of the relationship with speech and language. It is obvious that the more severe the loss the greater the effects. A simplified version of this is given in Figure 2.4.

Figure 2.4: Hearing loss in relation to language development (after Conrad, 1979)

Hearing loss	Characteristic language output
26-40 dB (mild)	Only 1,800-2,100 of 2,500 normally spoken words are uttered correctly.
41-70 dB (moderate)	Only 1,200-1,800 of the 2,500 words are spoken correctly. Words ending with 's' are the main problem.
71-90 dB (severe)	Only 200-1,200 of the 2,500 words are spoken correctly. In addition to plurals, unstressed words may be omitted; for example, 'Finished went home' may be uttered instead of 'When he was finished he went home'.

Typically work in a partially hearing unit is mainly in the area of speech training, hearing being boosted temporarily with the use of various types of hearing aids. However, the child's language is still undeveloped in terms of age of onset and complexity. Such oral education has been dominant within partially hearing units over the last twenty years. Many teachers consider aural-oral communication to be of prime importance, particularly as it helps the child to socialise with normally hearing children. With modern technology this can be achieved in many cases. This has restricted the use of manual sign language. However, in deaf clubs and in the playground signing is often used and can provide a language. Conrad (1979) argues that signing can be useful to the child, since the child acquires it quickly and easily.

Conrad goes on to develop the idea that deaf and partially hearing children are not a homogeneous population and that each child has the right to choose to think, to learn and be taught in the 'biologically preferred mode', i.e. signing. Such a change in policy would have quite an effect on the normal primary school teacher. However, as with the present situation, she or he must heed the specialist teacher and give the best circumstances for speech-reading (or lip-reading). If the partially hearing child was also taught to use signing then the class teacher would have to learn this also, which would be an added burden on the class teacher.

A second effect of hearing loss on the partially hearing child is that of the development of thinking which, in turn, affects learning and achievement. Early work in this area was carried out by Furth (1971); Furth and Youniss (1975). After conducting a number of experiments he found that concept formation was problematic in deaf children. The 'basic capacity to abstract and generalise' was not affected, but because of the lack of language certain concepts, such as the concept of opposite, were more difficult to acquire.

Conrad (1979) has raised the importance of the development of internal speech in relation to thinking. Internal speech is really speech for oneself, speech without vocalisation. In several ingenuous experiments Conrad was able to measure whether a deaf or partially hearing child had developed inner speech or not. He found that inner speech was related to the degree of hearing loss and the level of intelligence of the child. Children who had relatively higher scores in these areas had developed inner speech. More relevantly, those who had developed inner speech had better memory and had higher scores on reading and comprehension tests. It would seem then that it would be important to develop such inner speech, especially as the level of reading achieved by deaf children is quite low. By the time they leave school very few of them have a reading age above that of a nine-year-old hearing child and this 'does not permit complacency' (Conrad, 1979). Quite how such inner speech might be developed is a question for further research at the present time.

b) Auditory Discrimination

Many children who have speech and articulation difficulties beyond the age of seven or eight years also have problems with the discrimination of speech sounds (auditory discrimination). This is also reflected in poor reading, as noted by Clark (1970) and Harding (1983). In this latter piece of research children who had a specific reading disability were compared with a group of average readers. In this sample the correlation between speech errors (errors of articulation) and errors in auditory discrimination was 0.69. Auditory discrimination problems can occur in children who hear normally. None of the children in this study had apparent hearing problems.

Young children of three or four years of age often make errors in the discrimination of speech sounds, but they grow out of it. For example, my three-year-old son, whilst digging in the garden, called out, 'Look, a taddot'. Turning round, I replied, 'Oh yes, a taddot'. The response was a scornful look and the rejoinder, 'No, not a taddot, a taddot!' Most parents will remember such instances. The child could discriminate between the speech sounds produced by an adult in order to recognise some as incorrect. But it seems he could not discriminate between his own speech sounds, or why the scornful look?

Bailey (1978) points to three causes of faulty auditory discrimination. These are organic causes, learned immaturities and those occurring in the natural language of the child. Strictly speaking the third reason is not a cause of faulty discrimination but rather errors of natural language are speech difficulties. In the organic type of faulty auditory discrimination the problems are quite severe and the following pairs are difficult to discriminate: 'ck/g', 'b/p', 't/d'. When the child is simply immature the problem may be less severe. It is thought to be caused by lack of discrimination of sounds occurring in the home. For example, if there is a lot of background noise in the home or if speech is not used much.

When these difficulties occur in older school children (over seven years of age) the difficulties need proper assessment and remediation. Simple tests are provided by Wepman (1958) and McLeod and Atkinson (1972). Both tests present the child with spoken word pairs and the child has to say whether they are the same or different. For example, the tester may say 'crane/crane' or 'park/part' and the child responds same or different. The tests have been criticised because there are more different pairs than like pairs in the tests and therefore a child who prefers to respond 'different' will be more likely to be successful overall.

Remediation   Bailey (1978) advises on various activities which might improve auditory discrimination. Broadly speaking these fall into two categories which are listening games and phonic activity games. Learning Development Aids is one company which manufactures such games. Their Learning to Listen kit would be an example of a listening game. Games involving phonics are provided by the Stott Programme to give one example.

However, a resourceful adult can develop his or her own materials for training in auditory discrimination. Plastic containers holding peas, rice, sand and so on which make different sounds are useful. The equipment can be used for straight discrimination exercises or in games of sound lotto.

When we are considering the discrimination of speech sounds the remedial procedure is more difficult. Practice with producing rhymes: 'How many words can you think of which rhyme with fat?' 'Pam only likes food which rhymes with her name, so she likes...' Some times the teacher can read a story or rhyme which emphasises certain sounds and the children can learn appropriate phrases, such as 'Fee fi fo fum'. Many of the activities which are useful to assist in the development of auditory discrimination are also useful in the development of reading and are discussed in the next chapter.

DEVELOPMENTAL LANGUAGE DISORDER

Children who are backward in the understanding or production of language are usually either mentally retarded or partially hearing or deaf (Crystal, 1980). However, there are some children who do not have these problems but are nevertheless backward in language development. The problems are sometimes divided into receptive language problems (developmental and receptive dysphasia) in which the child exhibits difficulties in the understanding of language and expressive language problems (developmental dysarthria, developmental dyspraxia and developmental dysphasia), in which the child's problem is in the production of language. It may be useful to keep this distinction in mind, though in most cases the difficulties in one area will be only slightly more marked than difficulties in the other. For example, the child may have more of an expressive problem than a receptive problem. As Crystal points out, the classifications in terms of dyspraxia or dysarthria only serve to show the influence of the study of adult brain damage in the field of children's disorders. No such organic pathology can be shown in the case of children's problems and hence these labels do not serve any purpose.

Children who have only a receptive type problem are rarely seen as almost always lack of understanding of language leads to lack of ability to express oneself. According to Crystal, these children would have problems with auditory perception and discrimination (see earlier section) or auditory memory or auditory sequencing. This often shows itself in a difficulty with rhythms both in non-verbal (dancing and movement) and verbal expression.

The following conversation, described by Tough (1977), shows the language of a four-year-old child who does not seem to understand either the question being asked or the purpose of communication.

T.   What does he have for lunch?
C.   Dinner.
T.   Does he have dinner? What does he like best of all for dinner?
C.   Ah - dinner.
T.   He likes dinner. What do you like best of all for dinner?
C.   Dinner.
T.   What do you have? What does mummy put on the plate?
C.   Tea.
T.   She puts tea on the plate? What does she put on the plate for you to eat for your dinner?
C.   Tea.
T.   You think again. When you go home after the nursery, what does mummy put on the plate for dinner?
C.   Dinner.

The child also is backward in expression. For example, she used the phrase 'Them twos all my house' to mean 'These are all my houses'.

The teacher can make such simple observations of the child's language. In addition a check list, such as the Croydon Check List suggested by Wolfendale and Bryans (1978), may be useful.

There are other children (about one third) whose problem is primarily an expressive one. The actual content and grammar of the language the child uses is very poor. Crystal (1980) gives the example of a four-year-old child who understands speech very well, and whose hearing and auditory discriminations are normal, but his language is very poor, as shown below:

T.   There's a teddy bear, yes.
C.   Teddy at home.
T.   You've got one at home?
C.   Yeah.
T.   What do you call him?
C.   A teddy bear.
T.   Has he got a name?
C.   Yeah, he name.
T.   What is it?

```
C.      Er...
T.      What's his name?
C.      Teddy bear.
T.      Do you keep him in your bedroom?
C.      Yeah.
```

In some ways this child appears like the previous case cited, but he does attempt to answer the questions, even though the answers are very abbreviated.

The following example of Tough's is also mainly an expressive problem and is given to illustrate the many immaturities in the language. Tough recognises two kinds of immaturity; babyisms (using expressions such as 'gangan' for 'grandad', 'horsey' for 'horse') and lack of agreement of tense (e.g. 'thems twos all my house'; 'what them'). The following is an extract of a conversation held with a four-and-a-half-year-old child when looking at a picture book.

```
T.      Shall I show you some more of my nice toys
        in here? What are these?
C.      That's - what them?
T.      What is it?
C.      A pig.
T.      A pig. What's this?
C.      Ducky bag.
        ......
T.      You know what that is. What is it?
C.      Eh...No man.
T.      Oh it is a snowman, yes.
C.      No man again.
T.      And another snowman.
C.      (unintelligible)
T.      How many snowmen are there?
C.      Four, six, four, eight, four.
```

The teacher can make such observations of the child's speech and language accurately. Such items as appear on the language check list given previously may help with this.

According to Crystal (1980) it would then be necessary to get a more accurate description of the language being used. This would be a phonological analysis of the type used by Ingram (1976) or a grammatical description of the type used by Crystal, Fletcher and Garman (1976) and Garman (1980). Garman guards against vocabulary counting as a substitute for such analysis as estimates of normality vary widely (between 2,000 and 10,000 words for a five-year-old). In the recommended analyses it is necessary to grade the

acquired sounds and grammatical structures and compare
them with the stages of development of normal language.
A brief list of the appearance of certain grammatical
structures is given by Crystal (1980) and is presented
below as a rough and ready guide.

Figure 2.5: Stages in the acquisition of language (after
Crystal, 1980)

Age	Examples of speech	Description
16 months	Daddy/gone/there/no/milk	One word
21 months	Daddy there/see mummy/want book/where teddy	Two word Pivot and open
24 months	Want that car/my mummy gone)	
27 months	Mummy play ball/want more milk in there)	Elongation
30 months	Daddy gone town in car/me want more those)	of phrase
36 months	Daddy gone in garden and he did fall over/You pick that ball up 'cos it's nice	Two linked phrases

Similarly, the child's speech structures can be
compared with normal speech structures to see whether the
child's language is simply delayed (like a younger
child's but normal) or deviant (language has different
characteristics from the normal). This is a complex
question and requires very careful analysis. In the area
of phonology, one way in which deviancy may show up is in
the child's use of sounds to construct meanings. For
example, if the child is trying to say the words 'cup'
and 'cut' he needs to show in his speech that these are
separate words. Often young children who cannot
articulate 'p' and 't' would use the same sound 'p' to
terminate the word. A young child or one with delayed
language development might show homonyms in his language,
that is words which sound the same but mean something
different. Often children resolve this by using a
slightly different sound, even if it is not the normal
one used (he might say 'cup' and 'cups', for example).
Children with deviant language development do one of two
things; it seems like they use different sounds
inconsistently or they have multiple homonyms.
      Ingram (1976) gives the example of Jennifer (4:4,
i.e. 4 years and 4 months of age) to illustrate this
problem. She has problems with saying 's' in a

'tockings' usually. On occasion, however, she pronounces 'spoon' as 'fu', and 'Snoopy' as 'stoopy'. Often she drops the final consonant of a word; 'leaf' pronounced as 'nee', 'month' as 'mon', 'fish' as 'fi'. But sometimes she gives another sound for the dropped one, for example in 'knife' pronounced as 'nise', 'bath' as 'waf', and so on. In other words, her deviant speech shows many inconsistencies.

In contrast, Aaron (3:11) has many homonyms in his speech. For example, 'butter', 'ladder', 'letter', 'spider', 'water' and 'whistle' are all called 'dado'. Rather, obviously such deviant language results in unintelligibility and needs a high level of analysis by a speech therapist in order for progress to be made.

The third aspect of the child's language which needs to be studied before adequate remediation can be planned, is the nature of the child's system of communication. Whether the child engages in conversation spontaneously or not, whether he or she answers questions or imitates well. In other words, the therapist must ascertain what aspects of the child's communication system can be capitalised on in order to carry out therapy. This type of analysis is obvious in the work of Blank and Solomon (1972).

It must be obvious that language problems are extremely complex and children need to be seen by a properly qualified speech therapist.

Remediation   There are various materials and procedures available which a classroom teacher can use in order to assist language development however. There are language programs directed especially towards the under fives, such as The Renfrewshire Preschool Project (Donachy, 1975, 1976). Blank and Solomon (1972) based their language programme on the hypothesis that behind the language deficit was a deficit in the symbolic system for thinking. Language was not used by children to organise thought. So, in their language training, children were encouraged to think and to use language to explain their thoughts. One way of doing this was to get the child to develop a simple cause-and-effect model. In one session a child, Julie, was chalking with green chalk on the blackboard and was about to rub it out with a damp sponge. The conversation went something like this:

Teacher (Holds sponge down): If I lift the sponge up, what colour is going to be on the sponge?

31

```
Julie:     White.
Teacher:   Why white?
Julie:     Green.
Teacher:   Tell me why you said green?
Julie:     'Cause I wipe it off.
Teacher:   What did you wipe off?
Julie:     The green colour.
Teacher:   Let's see if you're right. (lifts sponge)
           Green! You're right. Very good.
```

Apparently, the discussion went on to cover the effect of sponge on rubbing out different colours, how to get chalk out of a sponge, use of board rubbers, etc. The main purpose here then is to develop the use of language in thinking. This is often emphasised in the natural development of language in preschool children, as language is used to convey thoughts in adult-child communication.

Research by Tizard and Hughes (1984) on the ways young children learn to communicate at home gives some insight into the factors affecting language development in preschool children. Many of the mothers in the study who were good at developing language showed the following features:

1. More frequent use of language for complex purposes (such as explaining why the fence fell down).

2. Use of a wide vocabulary.

3. Giving children a wide range of information (not just home-based).

4. Frequent taking on of a role in imaginative play.

5. Giving adequate answers to 'why' questions.

Many of these emphasise language use not only for communication but for thinking. By using language in reasoning and answering 'why' questions an adult is fostering thinking. Also the adult is extending the child's experience and providing a language model by extending the child's vocabulary and by playing with him or her. The following is an example of good language skill development by a mother, but it could just as easily be a teacher.

Conversation between mother and James (aged 3:6 years).

Mother (helping James to change):   There we

                    are...There-one slipper on.
James: I can see a bird.
Mother: A what, love?
James (watching bird in garden): See a bird.
Mother: Is there? Outside? (whispers)
James: Yes. (whispers)
James (points to bird): See. (whispers)
Mother: Is he eating anything? (whispers)
James: No. (whispers)
Mother: Where? (whispers throughout)
Mother: Oh yes, he's getting-Do you know what
           he's doing?
James: No. (whispers)
Mother: He's going to the...the...paper sack to
           try to pick out some pieces-Oh he's got
           some food there.
           And I expect he'll pick out some pieces
           of thread from the sack to go and make
           his nest...up...underneath the roof,
           James.
           Wait a minute and I'll-OK wait a mo' wait
           a mo' James.
James: That bird's gone. (whispers)
Mother: Has it gone now?
James: Yes. (whispers)
Mother: Oh.
           Take those long trousers off because
           they're...a bit muddy in there.
James: Yes he's gone.

Kits and materials are available but especially
recommended are the small kits developed by Learning
Development Aids, which are directed towards developing
specific skills, for example the use of prepositions.

SPEECH PROBLEMS

The sound structure of language is defined by phonetics
and phonology. Phonetics refers to the sound quality of
speech (that is, voice) which involves pitch and
loudness, whereas phonology refers to the speech sounds
themselves. Partially hearing children would be likely
to have difficulties with the voice whereas the ordinary
school child is more likely to have difficulties with
articulation of particular sounds. In addition, there
would be children who have problems with the motor
aspects of speech production, the stammerers and
stutterers.
So three types of speech problems are usually

identified. These are problems of voice, articulation difficulties and stammering and stuttering. Obvious examples of children with a voice problem, apart from the partially hearing, are children with Down's Syndrome who have a characteristically thick and deep voice. Problems with articulation are more common and it seems that the child has a babyish language, for example saying 'wabbit' for 'rabbit'. Stuttering, stammering and cluttering can take many forms. The most common is when the child repeats a word or sounds. The sounds 'h' and 's' seem to present the most difficulty as in the child who is asked 'How old is your brother?' and replies 'He's, he's, he'-s---f-f-f-four'.

When considering a child with such speech difficulties, it is important to ask whether the speech is really abnormal or whether the child will 'grow out of it' fairly soon. Strictly speaking, all cases of speech difficulty should be referred to the speech therapists, who have a wide range of tests and experience. Far too often, however, there is a long waiting list and, even if the child is supposed to be receiving speech therapy, he may not because of difficulties with taking the child to the therapist. Children with minor difficulties may not receive speech therapy simply because the speech therapist has too many children with severe problems to attend to. In these cases the ordinary classroom teacher can be of some help in the way to be described.

a) Difficulties with the Voice

Many very young children use their voice incorrectly, often speaking in a high voice, or in a monotone or shouting. According to Crystal (1980) there are many ways in which voice problems are classified. One classification might be based on types of damage to the vocal chords, another on disease pathology and another on the types of voice produced.

The actual characteristic changes in voice may be in pitch (high, low or monotone), loudness or timbre (tonal quality). The first two are least commonly affected though Tough (1977) gives an example of a child who is excessively quiet. Most of the abnormalities seen are in the area of timbre. The breathiness of the asthmatic child, the hypernasality of the child with chronic nasal congestion and the hoarseness of the child with laryngitis would all be examples of such abnormality. Although it is possible for such difficulties to be psychogenic in children the cause is nearly always organic.

Voice problems which are other than transient

should be referred to the child's parents and doctor. Occasionally the teacher may be asked to help in the treatment of the child. For example, operant conditioning may be used to reduce shouting or to encourage the child to talk louder. To do this, behaviourist principles are used, for example, if the child is talking too softly. The child is rewarded for each slightly louder sound with encouragement and praise. Non-audible sounds are ignored. Gradually the child talks a little bit louder and the loudest of the repertoire of sounds is rewarded. This little-by-little approach encourages the child and his normal speech becomes gradually louder. Such techniques may be used to reduce breathiness in asthma sufferers.

b) Stuttering and Stammering

Stuttering, or stammering (as some people prefer to call it), often appears in early childhood. Usually the child will have developed speech normally and then began stuttering. Andrews and Harris (1964) find 79% of the children they studied had some fluent speech (or, in some cases, a long period of fluent speech) before they became stutterers. The child's speech has characteristic repetitions of sounds, stops, gaps and so on which Crystal (1980) has classified into seven types, which are:

1. An abnormal amount of segment, syllable, word or phrase repetition - 'the pol-pol-policeman', 'the c-c-cater-p-pillar'. Certain sounds, in particular the fricatives (f,v,s) and plosives (p,k,d) present the greatest difficulty.

2. Obstruction of the air flow - referred to as blocking.

3. Abnormal prolongation of sound segments, as in 'f-f-fish'.

4. Introduction of extra words or sounds - 'um' or 'tut'.

5. Erratic stress patterns in words, mainly due to very hesitant speech.

6. Words left unfinished.

7. Awkward circumlocutions in order to avoid saying certain words which produce difficulty.

Such difficulties are also seen in normal non-fluency. It is normal for adults to hesitate occasionally, just as the normal speech of a three-year-old sounds like stuttering. But the period of repetition of sounds does not last long. Crystal gives an extract from a three-year-old:

'...and-and-my daddy did-did fall off the ladder and he-he-he did hurted his knee.'

An account of a stammerer is given by Tough (1977) of a boy, David, aged five. David is talking about his brother, who does not come to school.

'No, he-er-he doesn't, he doesn't. He's a, he's a, he's not, he's only, he's only, he's only, he's only-little. He's, he's, he's, he's, he's-four.'

This stammer is quite severe, showing repetition of syllables, words and phrases, introduction of extra sounds ('er', and later on 'Mm') and blocking.

Cluttering is a hurried and consequently unintelligible form of speech. It is described by Van Riper (1973) as 'characterised by slurred and omitted syllables, by improper phrasing and pauses due to excessive speed'. The speech is without rhythm and the breathing jerky, because in his hurry the child omits sounds, telescopes sounds and displaces sounds (for example malapropisms, such as 'Crise Rispies'). Some of these children who begin with speech disorders at about four years of age try to slow their speech down and eventually become stutterers.

The characteristics of stuttering change as the child develops. In a series of articles written in 1960 Bloodstein describes the development of stuttering in four phases. Phase one occurs mainly in pre-school children. The dysfluency occurs only from time to time, usually when the child is under some 'communicative pressure'. For example, he may be excited or wish to tell something to the teacher. Many children who have these problems do not become stutterers. As the studies of Andrews and Harris (1964) and Morley (1957) show, spontaneous remission is common in young children up to the age of six or seven years. Some children, however, pass on to Bloodstein's phase two, where the stuttering occurs in most of the child's speech. The stuttering usually occurs with content words and not so much with words at the beginning of a sentence, which was the case with younger children. Phase three is fully developed stuttering 'without the avoidance of speech'. Many of the other features of stuttering appear, for example, filling pauses with a sound, facial contortions, blocking or circumlocutions. This phase may appear in a child as young as eight years of age with the child being aware that he is a stutterer and being very annoyed by it, without the avoidance of speech. With phase four the emotional aspects become more severe, with the child exhibiting fear and embarrassment and avoiding communication. Whether such emotional aspects are the result or the cause of stuttering is of course a matter for debate, there being no accepted theory of the causation of stuttering. This is reviewed by Crystal (1980).

Van Riper (1973) has made an extensive study of stutterers, including forty-four longitudinal studies, and disagrees with the division of stuttering into phases as he does not see step-like changes. Instead he proposes four tracks of development, which describe 'common patterns of progressive change'. Some children seem to follow one track and some another. The phases of development of Bloodstein are similar to Van Riper's track one children. Another cause of development (Van Riper's track three) would be when a child begins to stutter following a traumatic incident. Typically the child is highly aware of his stuttering and is very anxious about talking. Apart from the usual repetitive features the child's speech is slow and careful, has many blocks and much tension is evident from the jaw jerks, gasping and facial contortions which the child exhibits.

The majority of childhood stutterers do not react adversely to stuttering however. They do not pass through to Bloodstein's phase four. Woods (1984) studied forty-eight stuttering boys (aged eight to twelve years) and their classmates in terms of speaking competence and social performance. The stutterers were considered poor talkers by themselves and their fluent classmates, but the two groups did not differ in terms of social performance. The disfluency can be ignored by junior school children though in adolescence it becomes a source of embarrassment and self-consciousness (Dalton and Hardcastle, 1977).

Remediation One of the main problems in the treatment of stuttering is deciding just what is the root cause of the problem. In some cases the stutter is the result of a traumatic event, and anxiety the underlying problem. In others anxiety may arise in self-consciousness about the stutter. Some theorists then believe in treating the

stutter directly whilst others would prefer to treat
other problems (anxiety and difficulties in the home).
There is an additional difficulty in treating young
childhood stutterers. That is the fact that the stutter
may be temporary and any treatment of it may emphasise
the stutter so that the child becomes aware that he is
stuttering. Some theorists then believe that stuttering
in young children should be left well alone.

Van Riper (1973) has made an extensive study of the
treatment of stuttering. In talking about the treatment
of very young stutterers he contrasts Western approaches
(typically American and British) with Eastern approaches
(typically Russian). The Western approach is to treat
the child through the parents, by encouraging the child
to communicate, relieving anxiety and preventing
emotional upset. The stutter is never worked on
directly. In the rest of Europe and the USSR treatment
is likely to be through speech training, with the stress
on rhythmical activities. Van Riper himself would treat
the beginning stutterer by providing models of fluency,
and using conditioning techniques to improve fluency and
desensitise the child to stuttering-producing or
anxiety-producing situations.

Treatment of the older established stutterer may be
much like an adult stutterer. According to Dalton and
Hardcastle (1977) treatment may consist of one of three
types. These are training alternative speech patterns,
relaxation and reduction of stuttering speech and
treatment by inhibition of disruptive elements. i)
Alternative speech patterns Taking the training of
alternative speech patterns first, this has been the most
popular method in recent years. The child's attention is
taken away from his own speech, thus allowing that speech
to develop differently. Therapy may take the form of
delayed auditory feedback (allowing the child to hear his
speech some time later) or masking (playing alternative
noise into his ears whilst he is speaking). A
development of this is in the practise of syllable-timed
speech, as described by Brandon and Harris (1967). In
this the child is asked to speak to a slow rhythmical
beat and this speech, though unusual, is fluent (without
stutter). Prolonged speech is a development of this
using delayed auditory feedback. The speech of the child
is played back to the child one-fifteenth or one-tenth of
a second later, thus producing prolonged fluent speech.
Over time the time of delay can be reduced or the
apparatus dispensed with to produce more normal fluent
speech (Ryan and Van Kirk, 1974).

ii) Relaxation techniques Relaxation techniques
concentrate on modifying and reducing the stutter and

relieving anxiety about the stutter. In therapy the stutterer is encouraged to gain control over his stutter. Irwin (1972) maintains that if the first syllable of a stammered word is drawn out, then it can be said more easily, with fewer repetitions and less tension. iii) Inhibition of disruptive elements The third form of therapy is perhaps the most ambitious. Van Riper's (1973) method is an amalgamation of relaxation and counter conditioning techniques are used to reduce anxiety. Then masking, delayed auditory feedback and reinforcement techniques are used to produce 'a new slow motion form of fluent stuttering' which may be modified further.

Some researchers prefer to treat the anxiety and avoidance of speaking shown by established stutterers. In young children this may take the form of play therapy and parental counselling. This aspect of the work becomes more important as the child approaches adolescence. In fact, some therapists concentrate on the self-concept of the stutterer and its modification (Fransella, 1972; Johnson, 1939).

Cluttering is a less common phenomenon than stuttering, but nonetheless may require treatment. Weiss (1964) advocates the use of syllable timed speech, rhythmical tapping, shadowing exercises and other exercises based on reading, which give practice in slow speaking.

From the above discussion of remedial techniques in fluency it is evident that many of these require the considerable expertise of the speech therapist. The class teacher can of course assist in this by following the therapist's specific recommendations and, in the young child at least, encouraging communication and relieving anxiety. The recitation of rhymes and singing of songs is also helpful to the stutterer, as these provide fluency by giving the child alternative rhythms.

c) Problems with Articulation

If a teacher suspects that a child's speech is abnormal, he or she will observe and give instances of that poor speech. But suppose the child has only a few poorly articulated sounds. How does the teacher decide whether the child should be referred or not? Two pieces of information are valuable to the teacher in this position. Firstly, he or she can refer to normal speech development and the timing of it and, in addition to direct observation, he or she can apply a simple test.

Ingram (1976) gives a table of the average age of

acquisition of English speech sounds, which is reproduced
here (Table 2.2). From this it can be seen that 90% of
children would have acquired the ability to produce most
sounds by age seven or eight. The most difficult sounds
to reproduce are 'z', 'th' as in 'the' and 'thing', 'v',
'j', 'c' as in 'ceiling', 's' as in 'sausage', 'r' and
'l'.

Table 2.2: Average age estimates for the acquisition of
English sounds, in years and months (after Ingram, 1976)

Sounds	Median age of customary use	Age of 90% of subjects
p,m,h,n,w	1:6	3:0
b	1:6	4:0
k,g,d	2:0	4:0
t,ing	2:0	6:0
f,y	2:6	4:0
r,l	3:0	6:0
s	3:0	8:0
ch,sh	3:6	7:0
z	4:0	7:0
j	4:0	7:0
v	4:0	8:0
th as in teeth	4:6	7:0
th as in the	5:0	8:0
z as in measure	6:0	8:6

The position of a sound in a word may also be
important. Renfrew (1966) gives the order of appearance
of final consonants for children with speech problems
(Table 2.3). This is similar to that for normal children
according to Ingram. From the table it would appear that
the correct articulation of 'k' and 'g' in the final
position is the most difficult, followed by the
fricatives ('f','th','s','v' and 'z') and 't'. Problems
with these sounds in the final position do not normally
persist after the age of four. Also, most children at
this age can articulate two or three consonants together
(as in 'train', 'spring'). Polysyllabic words can present
more difficulty and some of these are included in speech
therapists' tests (e.g. 'Christmas', 'toothbrush'). These
present a difficulty not only because of the number of
consonantal blends, but the ordering of them. Children
with speech problems often get the order wrong and call,
for example, 'teapot', 'peatot'.
    Children exhibiting speech problems do not simply
omit the sound but substitute one sound for another, e.g.

'toat' for 'coat', 'wabbit' for 'rabbit', 'chimley' for 'chimney', which may present a difficulty for the listener.

Table 2.3: Stages in the appearance of final consonants (based on Renfrew, 1966)

Stages 1-3	No final consonants.
4	Appearance of many final consonants.
5	Appearance of 'n', 'ing'.
6-7	'p', 'b', 'd' used finally and often to replace 't', 'k', 'g'.
8	Find 't' used. Fricatives attempted.
9	All final consonants except 'k', 'g'.
10	Articulation normal.

Some excellent examples of children's problems with articulation are given on Joan Tough's videotape of children with speech problems, produced as part of the School's Council Series on language development. She gives the example of Lynn, aged four years, who has difficulty with the 'd' in 'dinner' (pronounced 'tinner'), the 's' in 'sausage' and 'Susan' (pronounced 'so-age' and 'tusan') and the 'h' in 'house' (pronounced ''ouse'). Another child Fiona, aged four and a half, also has difficulty with 'h' in 'hedgehog' (pronounced ''edgeog'), the 'tt' in 'little' (pronounced 'likkle'), the 'th' in 'them' and 'that' (pronounced 'dem' and 'dat') and the 's' in 'snowman' (pronounced 'nowman').

These children's problems may appear quite severe, but they are quite young and, if speech therapy is sought early enough, the problems should be overcome.

If a child has been observed to mispronounce words, the teacher may want to apply a simple test to see whether the child's speech is very abnormal. Such a simple test was devised by Sheridan (1945) and used by Pringle et al (1966) in the National Child Development Study (see Figure 2.6). Though it does not give a diagnostic assessment of the child's precise problems, as a speech therapist's test might do, it will indicate some of them.

Figure 2.6: Sheridan's Speech Test

Say after me
Mary had a little lamb (practice)

1. Carol threaded a needle with wool.
2. She mended her sister's frock.

41

3. Roger grasped a bundle of sticks.
4. Eating porridge gives him strength.
5. My brother rode his bicycle to school.
6. Philip had scrambled eggs for breakfast.

Pringle et al (1966) found that most seven-year-olds could articulate all of these words correctly.

Many children's speech problems will be overcome with time. For, as Renfrew points out, many sounds are not substitutions but distortions. The 's' sound may not be quite accurate because the tongue is too far forward and the result is something like 'th'. Similar problems occur with 'r' where the tongue has to be far up in the roof of the mouth. If it is not the sound is something like 'w'.

Treatment   Therapy for articulation problems is normally carried out by a speech therapist. However if the child is young and the problem is not too severe the teacher or parent can give valuable assistance.

Specific therapy can be given in the form of correctly positioning the tongue, by demonstration, and practising the problem sound for prolonged periods at the beginning of words ('f-f-f-fish'). In addition, stories and rhymes which contain problem sounds can be very useful. For example, 'Mary, Mary, Quite Contrary' may be a good rhyme to use in the early stages. Tongue-twisters, such as 'She sells sea shells on the sea shore', should be left for more practised tongues.

SUMMARY

Language is a subject which is vastly expanding, both academically and in terms of treatment. Speech therapy requires a professional training which incorporates a degree these days. Yet many children with speech and language problems are not being treated at the present time because of lack of resources. Parents and teachers (and others) can help these children and those already receiving treatment perhaps with the assistance of the contents of this chapter.

3. READING DIFFICULTIES

One of the major problems confronting educators today is the difficulty some children have in learning to read. Despite developments in methods of general and remedial education, between two and seven per cent of children of normal intelligence fail to learn to read. This estimate of between two and seven per cent is broad, as the incidence of reading problems varies according to the way reading problem is defined. There are concepts of reading problem which warrant definition. Firstly, there is the concept of illiteracy. An illiterate person is defined as 'one who is unable to read or write his or her own language' (Encyclopaedia Brittanica), and is usually taken to refer to any person with a reading age below seven years. Semi-literacy refers to reading age between seven and nine years, and backwardness where reading age is two years below chronological age.

There would seem to have been some general improvement in literacy over the years. According to Morris (1966) 30% of school leavers were backward, semi-literate or illiterate in 1952. In 1948 5% of eleven-year-olds were illiterate and 21% were semi-literate, but by 1970, 0.4% were illiterate and 15% semi-literate (Start and Wells, 1972).

Secondly, there is the concept of reading backwardness. A child who is backward in reading is one whose reading age is lower than his or her chronological age. The estimate might vary according to the degree of backwardness. For example, in the Isle of Wight study (Rutter, Tizard and Whitmore, 1970) the incidence of reading backwardness was given as 6.6% of nine- to ten-year-olds where the criteria of backwardness was that reading age was 28 months behind chronological age. This was a fairly strict criterion of backwardness. Where a less strict criterion is used the incidence would be greater, for example Clark (1970) gives the incidence of 15.3% of seven-year-olds where the criteria used was that reading quotient be less than 85%.

Thirdly, there is the concept of reading retardation which is the concept used by Pringle in her study of 11,000 seven-year-olds (Pringle, Butler and Davie, 1966). This concept relates to the concept of mental age, that is, where reading age is significantly below mental age then the child is retarded in reading.

In the National Child Development Study the incidence of reading retardation was given as 18%.

The concept of reading retardation is linked to the concept of specific reading disability. The term refers to a group of children of average or above average intelligence who, despite adequate school attendance and normal teaching, fail to learn to read. The Department of Education and Science, in the Tizard Report (1972), use the term specific reading disability:

> to describe the problems of a small group of children whose reading (and perhaps writing, spelling and number) abilities are significantly below the standards which their abilities in other spheres would lead one to expect.

(DES Report, 1972)

Though this term is relatively new, the recognition that reading problems occur in normal children 'despite conventional instruction, adequate intelligence and sociocultural opportunity' (McDonald Critchley, 1970) is not. Usually such children have been called children with specific dyslexia or developmental dyslexia. However, as discussed by Clark (1970) and in the Tizard Report (DES 1972) the terms seem to refer to children with similar, if not synonymous, problems. The term 'specific reading disability' is the term preferred by the Tizard Report (DES, 1972) and the Warnock Report (1978).

Nevertheless, the term 'specific reading disability' is not an exact one. It can refer to reading backwardness of two years in relation to chronological age in children of normal intelligence. As given by Clark (1970) the incidence is then 6.3% of nine-year-olds. A stricter criterion gives a smaller figure. For example, Rutter, Tizard and Whitmore (1970) give the incidence of 3.7% of children where reading backwardness is 28 months behind the level predicted from age and IQ. Some researchers adopt a sliding scale, so that backwardness of six months in six-year-olds is seen as indicative of specific reading disability, but the backwardness has to be two years or more in nine-year-olds (Lyle, 1969). Other researchers (e.g. Pavladis, 1982) introduce the concept of class in the definition of specific reading disability or dyslexia. The child is required to come from a good middle class home to warrant being called dyslexic. Hence the concepts of specific reading disability and dyslexia vary slightly, and so accordingly do estimates of incidence.

Another factor which might affect incidence is the age of the children. Owen, Adams, Forrest, Stolz and Fisher (1971) looked at the number of children aged five to fifteen years who needed remedial help, and found that this was 2% of the total population of school children, but within this group the majority (67%) were in the age range eight to eleven years. However, despite the variation in estimates of the incidence of specific reading disability, it would still seem to be useful to see children with specific reading disability as distinct from children with general backwardness, as the question of why children of average intelligence should have reading problems is still an unanswered one.

THE CLASSIFICATION OF READING DISABILITY

Any classification of reading disability must take into account those problems encountered by children who are backward readers and those who have a specific reading disability. The distinction is linked to ideas regarding the causality of reading disabilities as many would give environmentalist explanations for reading backwardness and neurological or maturational lag type explanations for specific reading disability. Theories of the causality of reading disability will be examined first. A second important area which has some bearing on the classification of reading disabilities is the explanation of the reading task itself. Thirdly, research on the adult dyslexias and alexias may be of relevance.

Theories of Causality

Broadly speaking, there are three theories about the causality of reading disability, though more modern theories recognise the complexity and multiplicity of factors in causality.

The three major viewpoints referred to are organic / neurological explanations, functional explanations including developmental lag and environmentalist explanations.

Organic/neurological Explanations. One of the first researchers into reading disability was Hinshelwood (1917) who described three types of word blindness in adults which were due to damage in certain areas of the brain. One of these types was very common and formed the basis of his theory concerning congenital word blindness in children.

Later Hermann and Norrie (1958) also equated

children with a reading disability with brain damaged adults with Gerstmann's Syndrome where right-left confusion problems with finger localisation and writing problems are evident. Their ideas were further extended by Kinsbourne and Warrington (1966) who considered that there were two types of children with specific reading disability - the Gerstmann group and the language group. More up-to-date research on the various types of dyslexia or specific reading disability is discussed later, but it could be that some types of reading disability have a neurological basis and others not.

A problem with auditory-visual integration was first described by Birch and Belmont (1965) and forms the basis of a neurological theory put forward by them and Geschwind (1964). As integrative and associative functions of an auditory-visual nature are normally localised in the inferior parietal region, a congenital defect in this area could account for reading disability. A more up-to-date discussion of the possible involvement of the inferior parietal region is given by Beech (1985).

A fairly recent neurological theory has been put forward by Witelson (1977). She maintains that dyslexic children have a different kind of hemispherical dominance or laterality pattern due to a neural deficit. The theory attempts to account for the differing incidence of reading disability in boys when compared with girls, there being something like four boys to every one girl with a reading problem. Specifically she maintains that dyslexic boys have cerebral hemispheres which both function as if they are right hemispheres, so they are good at form and colour perception but poor at language.

Functional Approaches. Samuel Orton, who worked in the 1920s and 1930s, is renowned for his ideas concerning the imbalance in the functioning of the two cerebral hemispheres. The problem was that the two hemispheres were often in conflict so that at one time the left hemisphere might recognise a letter and at another time the right hemisphere. As the right hemisphere recognised as identical mirror images of visual impressions received by the left hemisphere this led to letter confusions and reversals or, in Orton's terms, strephosymbolia (literally, twisted signs). In normal readers such a problem does not arise as the left hemisphere is functionally dominant.

Another development of the view that the brain of children with reading disabilities might function differently from normal children is given by the theory of maturational lag. Lauretta Bender's concept in the 1950s was based on the 'slow differentiation of (brain) pattern'. If the child with a reading problem is immature then this should be predictable from an early age. DeHirsch, Jansky and Langford (1967) attempted to do just that. Kindergarten children were tested and followed through to the end of second grade in primary school. They found that nine tests could be used to identify high risk children, that is children who would be likely to develop reading problems.

In more recent times Satz and Sparrow (1970) have expanded the theory of maturational lag. They maintain that the slow development of cerebral dominance might have different behavioural expressions at different ages. For example, hand dominance will be established in a four- or five-year-old, but not right-left awareness which normally develops at about eight or nine years of age. Maturational lag might show itself in mixed hand dominance in a young child, but not an older child with reading problems as he or she will have outgrown this area of difficulty. The older dyslexic child is likely to have more problems in the language and conceptual areas. The theory has been verified to some extent by Satz, Taylor, Friel and Fletcher (1978) and Leong (1976) and the theory is discussed in greater detail by Downing and Leong (1983).

Environmentalist Explanations. Merrit (1972) suggests that neurological and other theories which maintain that reading disability is constitutional in origin are very little use since:

> in the case of every factor that is supposed to contribute to a reading disability we can find a child who should be at risk, but who can read perfectly well.

Merrit suggests that various unfortunate circumstances effect the child's learning. For example, the child may have been taught to sound out letters, but when he applies this process to some words it is inappropriate, so he abandons the idea. Other circumstances, for example the teacher not being available to reinforce correct responses, may also play their part. But eventually the child may respond to the situation by developing a reading neurosis. Then anxiety makes learning even more difficult. To do him justice Merrit does not claim that all children with reading problems have difficulties of this nature, but they account for about 20% of the children. It is almost self-evident that most children who have become failing readers (even if there is some constitutional cause) are also very anxious about the problem.

Factors associated with the school environment have also been mentioned by Morris (1966), Chall (1967) and Rutter, Tizard and Whitmore (1970). Clark (1970) in a study of backward readers seemed to suggest that factors in the home environment could account for reading failure. Specifically, there was a lack of:

> active assistance on the part of the parents, though the parents were positive in their attitude towards school. Most of the children came from large families and the reading material seemed to be mainly that supplied by the school.

In a subsequent study of preschool children who could read, Clark (1976) found that children who read early had parents who themselves enjoyed reading and who were involved with the child in his education. So it would seem that the environment plays its part, as will be evidenced in some of the remedial suggestions.

Theories of Reading

One of the most comprehensive theories of reading is that given by Gibson (1965), Gibson and Levin (1975). She describes learning to read as a three step process, which are:

1. Learning to differentiate graphic symbols.

2. Learning to decode letters to sounds.

3. Using progressively higher order units of structure.

These steps, though roughly sequential, also overlap. Gibson and her colleagues have shown by a series of experiments that the ability to differentiate graphic symbols makes rapid progress between the ages of four and eight. From ages five or six years the child begins to recognise letter-to-sound correspondences (or grapheme-phoneme correspondences as they are more accurately called). As the child gets more proficient he or she learns to read 'chunks' of graphic stimuli at a single fixation. Gibson believes that the smallest chunks correspond to spelling patterns. That is, words can be perceived at a glance when they follow regular spelling patterns. At a higher level still there are chunks and phrases which follow certain syntactic and semantic patterns. Gibson thinks that reading is an adaptive process, in that the child gradually learns to adapt to the text.

Smith's (1978) theory of reading is rather different from Gibson's in that learning to read is seen as similar to learning the spoken language. The language of books is a different language from the spoken one and the child must recognise this fact. Once he does so he learns to 'read by reading' by getting the meaning out of passages. In some sense the child must pick out the visual features of words, but this is seen as relatively unimportant.

> Learning to read can be perceived as making sense of more and more kinds of language in more and more contexts. Fundamentally a matter of experience. (Smith, 1978)

Whilst this account by no means exhausts theories of reading development it does give some account of the two major approaches. A skills model is provided by Gibson's theory and Smith's account typifies the psycholinguistic approach.

Dyslexia in Adults and Children

Research with the acquired alexias and dyslexias can give us some insight into the possible types of reading disability. Notable amongst the contributions has been Coltheart, Patterson and Marshall (1980) and Coltheart (1982). Coltheart has described four types of acquired dyslexia. These are:

1. Pure alexia or alexia without agraphia
   The patient cannot read but can write and spell by a letter-by-letter approach.

2. Phonological dyslexia
   In this the patient recognises whole words but cannot tell you the sounds of various letters and he or she cannot read non words.

3. Surface dyslexia
   The patient can read regular words (e.g. rub, steam, pure) but not irregular words (e.g. sew, yacht, steak, pint) and he or she can read regular non words (e.g. rad).

4. Deep dyslexia
   The patient can read concrete words (e.g. lamp, man) quite well but not more abstract words (e.g. lazy).

Coltheart maintains that surface dyslexia quite commonly occurs as a developmental problem, where a child has difficulty in learning whole word recognition though letter-to-sound correspondence rules one learnt quite well. Phonological alexia also occurs in children who have difficulty in learning letter-to-sound (or grapheme-phoneme) correspondence rules.

Subgroups of Developmental Dyslexia   The division of children with reading problems into groups with a different neurological or maturational basis for their defects has been popular for some time. Boder (1971) describes three groups, the dyseidetic group having visual problems (approximately 9% of dyslexics), the dysphonetic group having auditory and linguistic problems (about 63%) and a mixed group. The division into a visual and auditory group is also given by Johnson and Myklebust (1967) and to some extent by Kinsbourne and Warrington (1963) in their description of the Gerstmann group and a language group.

A rather different approach has been adopted by Vernon (1979) who described five types of retarded reader with reference to the reading problems encountered rather than the underlying deficit. The five types of retarded reader were children who were unable to:

a) analyse complex visual shapes
b) analyse whole words into phonemes
c) make regular grapheme-phoneme associations
d) grasp irregularities in grapheme-phoneme associations
e) group words into phrases and sentences.

Vernon goes on to say that some of these problems might be similar to those described by others, for example groups a) and b) might correspond to the visual and language groups defined previously.

But what evidence is there that there are subgroups of dyslexia? Are children with one type of reading difficulty distinctly different from children who appear to have different problems; or are they all fairly similar really? Petrauskas and Rourke (1979) attempted to solve this problem using a factor analytic approach. Four groups were identified which were:

a) Language disturbance including poor auditory-verbal memory and auditory-perceptual skills.

b) Sequencing difficulties both in language, number and visual-perceptual tasks. The children also had difficulties in finger localisation (finger agnosia).

c) Defects in conceptualisation especially where verbal coding and verbal reasoning is concerned.

d) This group was like group b), but without finger agnosia.

From this research it would appear that most dyslexic children have deficits in the language-verbal area. No visual perceptual problems are in evidence but this may be because the sample of children may have outgrown that particular problem in line with Satz and Sparrow's (1970) theory. Alternatively, they may not have sampled the group of children with visual deficits which is usually fairly small.

In contrast, Mattis, French and Rappin (1975) identified a visuospatial subtype. 90% of their 82 dyslexic children exhibited one of the three following syndromes:

a) Language disorder typified by difficulty in naming comprehension and speech.

b) Articulatory and graphomotor difficulties including sound blending.

c) Visuospatial difficulties. The children in this group had problems with visual memory and their verbal IQs were 10 or more points above performance IQ.

Similarly, Hicks and Spurgeon (1982) identified three important factors in a study of 180 dyslexic children. The problem areas were:

a) Auditory problems. Children had difficulties discriminating sounds and sound blending.

b) Verbal labelling. Children had difficulties with phonics, grapheme-phoneme correspondence left-right discrimination and vocabulary.

c) Visual problems. Children had difficulty with visual memory and labelling.

Whilst these last two pieces of research

demonstrate that visual-motor difficulties may occur in children with reading disability, there is little concordance in the other two groups. This may have been an artifact of the tests given, for example, one piece of research included a test of phonics whereas the other did not. Despite this there would seem to be at least more than one type of dyslexia or reading difficulty due to problems in the auditory-verbal and language area.

A Proposed Classification

With all the wealth of research into reading, it is still difficult to formulate a definite psychological classification of reading disability. There may be some degree of overlap in the types proposed by the various researchers, and it may be necessary to disregard the problem of causality and describe only the problems seen. This is in line with Vernon's (1979) proposal, though I would suggest a division into four groups as given below (see Figure 3.1). The problems are described at two levels. Firstly, specific reading or learning difficulties which cover problems in basic underlying skills. Secondly, there are higher order difficulties of a conceptual and linguistic nature.

Figure 3.1: Proposed classification of reading difficulties

Specific reading difficulties

    a)   Visual - motor difficulties
    b)   Auditory - verbal and language difficulties

Higher order reading difficulties

    a)   Auditory - visual integration and grapheme - phoneme correspondence.
    b)   Higher order conceptual and language problems.

It may be that younger children with reading difficulties are mainly of types a) and b) of specific reading difficulties which would be in line with Satz and Sparrow's classification. Also these two categories would be similar to Johnson and Myklebust's (1967) categories and others who divide dyslexias into visual and auditory types. Older children's difficulties are likely to show up in learning grapheme-phoneme correspondence and in reading using higher order language skills such as syntax and semantics.

SPECIFIC READING DIFFICULTIES

a) Visual-motor Difficulties

Bender (1957) was a pioneer in the work on visual-motor deficits in dyslexic children. She developed the Bender-Gestalt test to demonstrate such difficulties as drawing figures in the correct orientation, drawing an open or closed figure, drawing the correct number of lines or dots in a figure. An example of the difficulty a child might have in drawing such a figure is given in Figure 3.2. The child failed to draw a square, could not integrate figures properly (they do not touch) and often drew open instead of closed figures. Such severe problems are often noted in clinic samples of dyslexic children (Silver and Hagin, 1966; DeHirsch, Jansky and Langford, 1967).

Such visual-motor problems are seen in children referred to as visual dyslexics (Boder, 1971; Johnson and Myklebust, 1967) but the group is usually smaller than the group of auditory dyslexics (usually about 9 or 10% of the total group of dyslexics). The visual-motor deficit, whilst demonstrated by the Bender-Gestalt test, also shows itself in other ways. For example, the child is most likely to have higher verbal abilities than visual abilities. The child whose Bender-Gestalt test result is given in Figure 3.2 had a verbal IQ of 86. He was very poor at the block design test (that is, in copying drawings such as

with patterned cubes), and in the picture completion subtest (saying what is missing from a picture). Terence also had a problem which showed itself in his inability to discriminate reversed words from unreversed words. In one test he had to underline words which were the same as the first word in the line. He made several errors, as shown below:

| **burn** | <u>brun</u> burn bunr rubn <u>burn</u> |
| **dip** | pid <u>bip</u> <u>dip</u> dib <u>dip</u> |

The problem is often dubbed as a deficit in visual sequencing and has been found by researchers, including

Figure 3.2: Examples of Bender-Gestalt test performance from a) retarded reader age 8 years 3 months, and b) average reader age 8 years 1 month.

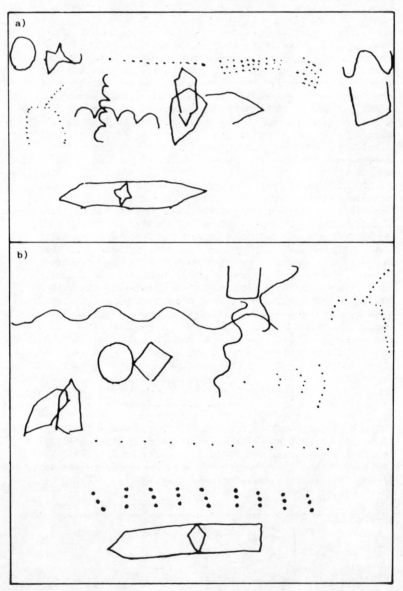

Doehring (1968). Sometimes this difficulty is reflected in the reading and spelling errors which the child makes. The child quoted above spelt words as though he was going by sound cues alone, and may not have made any judgements about the look of the word. For example, 'talk' was spelt 'tork', 'egg' was spelt 'oge'. This difficulty is elaborated further in the section on spelling. In reading this child had begun to make grapheme-phoneme correspondences, and so was beginning to decode words, but often the word read was not visually like the correct word, demonstrating that he was not using the shape of the word as a cue. For example, he read 'help' as 'hunt', 'white' as 'which'. Typically, as for other children with visual problems, he had many 'reversal' errors, reading 'for' instead of 'from', 'sum' instead of 'sun', spelling 'ball' as 'doll', 'top' as 'tob' etcetera.

Children with these visual-motor problems, visual-memory problems and reversal problems may have an underlying motor difficulty. Whilst not apparently clumsy, that is they may walk, run and get themselves dressed, they often have motor difficulties which are demonstrated by testing. One child, Nigel, had no gross motor difficulties, but had difficulty in tying shoe laces, placing pegs in a board, tracing a circle and so on. Such motor impairment has been shown in many children with reading difficulties by Lovell and Gorton (1968), and Rutter, Tizard and Whitmore (1970). These motor difficulties are discussed in greater detail in a later chapter.

Children with these severe difficulties have often been likened to adults with brain damage who exhibit the Gerstmann syndrome (Kinsbourne and Warrington, 1966). With such severe difficulties finger agnosia is often apparent. This is a problem in the awareness of the positioning of fingers. In one test the child is asked 'Close your eyes. Now, how many fingers am I touching? One or two?' The child may be unable to differentiate them by the sense of touch alone. This difficulty in young children was found to be most predictive of later reading difficulty (Satz and Sparrow, 1970).

Today research into reading has moved away from visual-motor problems. Many researchers, for example Vellutino (1980), Beech (1985), Bradley and Bryant (1985), consider such visual-motor difficulties as the result rather than the cause of reading difficulties.

There are some tests which the teacher can give to children which might help to indicate visual-motor difficulties. In particular, Daniels and Diack's

Standard Reading Tests (Diagnostic Tests 1, 2 and 4) would be of use, though they may add little more to the information gleaned from useful observation.

Remediation   Unfortunately very few of the recommendations given in this section have been critically tested.   Very little, if any, research has been carried out into the efficacy of these methods. However, there are several problem areas which may be considered in turn:

i)   Figure-ground perception. Difficulties with figure-ground perception is shown by the child who fuses letters (reading clown as down) or omits or adds letters. He or she may lose his or her place frequently, may omit whole lines when reading or may have to retrace. The problem rarely occurs in isolation.
    The child can be helped by having to analyse words into parts using cut out or plastic letters. In a less severe form, methods which emphasise letter differences are useful.   For example, colour cueing or kinaesthetic methods may help.
    Exercises in which the child has to distinguish figure from ground may also help.   Marianne Frostig includes some of these in her programme, an example being given below.   Exercises involving letters and words can also be given.

Exercises in figure-ground discrimination

ii)   Position in space and directionality. The child with reading difficulties often shows reversals and difficulty in differentiating right from left.
    When the child makes directional mistakes, for example reading 'was' for 'saw', 'left' for 'felt', the teacher can indicate in his book where to begin reading:

i.e.   ₓ<u>saw</u>

    For reversal problems reminder cards can be attached to the child's desk with picture and representative word.   For the 'b/d' discrimination a mnemonic can be taught as illustrated below:

bed

Exercises can be given to assist visual discrimination, for example, as given previously, the child has to underline words which are the same as the first word in the line. Presentation of these can be speeded up using a tachistoscope or, these days, a microcomputer. For example, the word 'apple' can be briefly shown and the child can be asked to find it amongst the array given:

amongst   little   ape   puddle   apple

These suggestions are mainly based on Johnson and Myklebust's (1967) work to whom the reader is referred for additional information.

iii) Spatial relationships and visual sequences. While Frostig's spatial relationships test is useful, difficulties in this area may be apparent from the child's reading or spelling ('gril' for 'girl', 'sitrng' for 'string').
Remedial exercises would tend to emphasise such sequences, for example, copying bead and pegboard patterns. Again tachistoscopic presentations of patterns may assist this. A word, for example train, is briefly presented and the child has to select amongst the following: trail larait train tain rain. Again, most of these suggestions are given by Johnson and Myklebust. Various materials for the development of visual sequential memory are also produced by Learning Development Aids.
There has been little research into the efficacy of these exercises in the development of perceptual-motor skills. Two studies (Bieger, 1974 and 1978) trained poor readers in those skills covered by the Frostig test over one school year. These skills were figure-ground perception, perceptual constancy, spatial relations, and visual sequencing. At the end of the year there was no significant difference in reading attainment between the children who received training and those who did other activities. However, it may be that the training was not carried out early enough. The Bradley and Bryant study on training in phonemic awareness (see next section) would seem to indicate that early training is very important as a preventative measure. This point is discussed in greater detail by Beech (1985).

iv)   Eye movement. Most adult readers only fixate once
or twice per line of writing, but children, when they are
learning to read, need to fixate each word sequentially.
Erratic eye movements can be observed by teachers, and if
the child also misreads word sequences a problem in this
area may be indicated.

Various kinds of markers can assist the reader here
and they can be graded in difficulty:

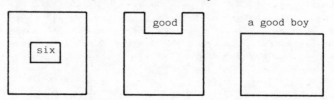

Various tracking exercises have been suggested by
Frostig and Maslow (1973).

v)   Motor difficulties. Any gross motor difficulties
shown by these children may be remedied by any of the
methods discussed in Chapter Five. In particular,
exercises for the development of body image and body
awareness would be recommended.

The method used in the teaching of reading to
children with visual-motor problems is discussed by some
researchers. A popular idea, initiated by Johnson and
Myklebust (1967) involves teaching through the intact
channel of communication, in this case the
auditory-verbal channel. The idea is that teaching
should capitalise on the strengths in that the child with
visual problems sometimes has good language and
auditory-verbal abilities. The child should then be
asked to read new words by thinking of others which might
sound the same and by guessing from context. The child
may be able to pick up grapheme-phoneme correspondences
quite early provided that visually easy words, for
example short words, are utilised in the initial stages.
At the same time it is advocated that the child is asked
to build up the weakness by carrying out some of the
exercises discussed here.

b) Auditory-verbal and Language Difficulties

Delay in language development, speech difficulties and
problems with auditory-verbal discrimination often seem
to be associated with reading difficulties. In a study

by Clark (1970) of nineteen children of normal intelligence who were severely backward in reading (over two years retarded) twelve showed poor auditory discrimination and ten had associated speech difficulties. In a study by the author (Harding, 1983) most children with specific reading difficulties had associated speech and language problems, though these were especially severe in working class girls with a reading disability. One typical example is given by Maria, an eight-year-old girl of average intelligence (WISC. IQ 105) who had very poor language skills. She was initially unable to retell a story, but eventually gave an account of the three little pigs which was only 91 words in length (the average length of story for average readers was 355 words). Although the story sequence was correct, the language was very poor in terms of vocabulary and sentence structure. She used the following phrases for example: '...but he couldn't blew down it', '...so the three little pigs lived in this thing after all'. Maria spoke with a gruff voice and several mistakes were made in speech. For example, when given Sheridan's articulation test (see language chapter) she repeated 'Roger grasped a bundle of sticks' as 'Roger grast a bungle of sticks', and repeated 'strength' as 'strench'. In contrast she made only one error on the Bender-Gestalt test and her motor skills were good for her age.

We might be tempted to think that her reading difficulties were caused by a poor environment as a visit to the home indicated material poverty and lack of books. When asked if Maria had any books, her mother produced a somewhat battered copy of The Three Little Pigs, and yet she could not tell this story effectively. Her auditory discrimination was also poor, for example in the Wepman test she thought the following pairs of words were the same, 'vow' and 'thou', 'shake' and 'shape', 'clone' and 'clothe'. Her reading age was very low at 5:4 years, and she had very poor knowledge of letter names and letter sounds.

Whilst a child with such obviously severe difficulties would benefit from language stimulation centred around books, there are also the difficulties with the discrimination between sounds and speech difficulties. Some of these are discussed in Chapter Two. If a teacher suspects problems in this area, for example if the child makes frequent errors of a particular kind (pronouncing 'sh' sounds as 's', 'c' as 't' and so on) then a test such as the Wepman Test (1958) or Domain Phonics Test (McLeod and Atkinson, 1972) may be given. If a more severe hearing loss is suspected then a qualified audiologist should test the child.

An additional complication may be that of auditory sequential memory. This is often shown by the WISC-R subtest of digit span in which the child has to repeat a series of numbers. The child Maria quoted earlier could only repeat three numbers forward and two backwards. A child of her age should be able to repeat four forwards and three backwards.

Sometimes children have additional difficulties with sound blending. This is where the child knows the sounds of letters, digraphs etcetera, but is unable to blend them to form words, e.g. he may be able to read 'sh-i-p', but he is unable to blend them to make the word 'ship'. Some children only have the problem when it comes to reading longer words as certain letter combinations are not read together. For example, 'sunlight' needs to be read as 'sun-light' or 's-un-l-ight', but certainly not by the child sounding out each letter. Sound blending can be tested by a subtest of the Illinois Test of Psycholinguistic Abilities or by supplementary test three of the Neale Analysis of Reading.

<u>Remediation</u>   Some of the more general policies regarding language development and speech remediation have been discussed in Chapter Two. However, with particular reference to reading, it should be remembered that the language of books is rather different from spoken language and the child must be familiar with this if he or she is to make progress in reading. The child should be read to and read with at every available opportunity, whether this be in the form of books, magazines or cereal packets.

Tizard, Schofield and Hewison (1982), in their research, showed just how important such reading is. They divided a group of retarded readers into two. One half, the experimental group, had parents who were encouraged by the researchers to read to and with their children. The other half, the control group, were given extra tuition in reading in the classroom. The experimental group was superior to the control group in reading at the end of the school year.

i) <u>Auditory discrimination</u>   More specific techniques are needed to remedy other problems. Auditory discrimination can be improved by the following methods suggested by Johnson and Myklebust (1967) and McCreesh and Maher (1974).

1. Match sounds. Have the child say a sound that can be

sustained (e.g. 'Mmmm') and have him raise his hand
when the teacher says one that is the same.

2. Encourage reauditorisation. This time the child has
    to say the sound to himself and say when the teacher
    says the same sound.

3. Utilising visual and kinaesthetic cues. Whilst the
    child is producing the sound he has to concentrate on
    the positioning of tongue, lips etcetera.

4. Chaining. Change one sound successively to form a
    new word. 'Cat-can-man-men-met-wet'.

5. Rhyming games. Go round a group of children asking
    each child to give a word that rhymes with the word
    just spoken. This can be adapted in the form of 'I
    went to market and bought a fan, man, can and pan'.

It is perhaps pertinent to note here that rhyming
is an ability which seems to be important in relation to
reading (Bradley and Bryant, 1978) and may be developed
in young children prior to going to school as it may be
an important precursor to learning to read (Bradley and
Bryant, 1985). Read (1971) has suggested a game which
should develop this important skill. The game is played
with puppets who only like objects which rhyme with the
puppet's name. For example, 'Pam likes jam and ham'. So
the teacher asks the child 'What animal would Pat like
for a pet, a cat or a dog?', 'What kind of weather does
Jane like, sunshine or rain?'

ii) Phonemic awareness   Training in phonemic awareness is
a specialised form of training in auditory
discrimination. In this the discrimination of speech
sounds or phonemes is stressed. An excellent piece of
research in this area is provided by Neuman (1981).
Children were given exercises in recognising the
similarity and differences in the phonemes at the
beginning, middle and end of words. For example, a child
might be asked, 'Do these words begin with the same sound
- man, mouse'. The children were also asked to look for
words that rhymed, for example 'moon' and 'spoon'. 256
first grade children were trained over a period of eight
months and improved in their ability to discriminate
phonemes compared with a control group who did
alternative exercises (mathematics and art projects).
Bradley and Bryant (1983) tested 400 children before they
had learnt to read. A small subset, i.e. children who

were poor at the discrimination of speech sounds were selected for further research. One group of children received training in phonemic awareness, by various exercises. One of these was to show the children pictures which had to be sorted according to their name, for example 'pan', 'man' and 'fan' would be placed together. Plastic letters were also used to reinforce this work with some children. Another group had sorting exercises also, but this did not involve sorting by phonemes, but rather according to colour and function. This served as a control group. Three or four years later the children who had been trained in phonemic awareness and the use of plastic letters were three or four months ahead in reading and spelling compared with the control group. So phonemic awareness seems to help reading development in children who are poor at this skill.

Whilst these children were not ones who were already poor readers it seems likely that training in phonemic awareness would also help their reading development. The Bradley and Bryant study does demonstrate that training in phonemic awareness could be a good preventative measure for children who are poor in this skill when they start school.

Children who have difficulties in the sequencing of sounds in words may respond to the following exercises:

i)   Ask the child to imitate rhythms and patterns by copying tapped patterns or musical rhythms using drums, bells and tambourines.

ii) Get the child to recognise the rhythmical sequence of words by drumming or tapping the rhythm. For example, tomato (.-.), Rebecca (..-.).

Sound blending can be taught using visual cueing, for example have the child recognise that certain words look the same in certain ways ('pit', 'fit', 'sit', 'mit'). Then split the words up and have the child imitate the sounds made by the teacher and gradually blend them.

Various commercially produced materials can be useful in the training of auditory-verbal skills. Sometimes these are total programmes, such as Goal produced by Learning Development Aids, but other structure kits have their uses, e.g. Sound Lotto (also produced by Learning Development Aids). Various phonics programmes, such as the Domain Phonics Programme (McLeod and Atkinson, 1972) and Alpha to Omega (Hornsby and Shear, 1980) are also useful in this area.

HIGHER-ORDER READING DIFFICULTIES

a) Auditory-visual Integration and Grapheme-phoneme Correspondence

One of the main skills that a reader has to acquire is the automatic knowledge that certain letters or letter combinations represent certain sounds. Even with the irregularity of English language it is the only way we can read unknown words without reference to another person. We break the word down into its constituent parts, sound out these parts and then blend them together. Such grapheme-phoneme correspondence rules, otherwise known as phonics, are necessary for reading. Harding, Beech and Sneddon (1985) demonstrated that this graphophonic ability increased dramatically between the ages of five and seven years. Children with a reading disability have very poor graphophonic ability when compared with normal readers (Harding, 1984). Clark (1970) also endorsed this when she commented:

> Clearly a number of backward readers had not yet learnt to recognise sound-symbol relationships, let alone reproduce it as required to spell correctly.

Such graphophonic skills may depend on an underlying ability to make auditory-visual associations. Birch and Belmont (1965) thought that this was the main underlying disability of backward readers and developed a test of this skill, known as the tapping test. In this the examiner taps a pattern with a pencil on the table and the child has to pick a visual pattern corresponding to the auditory stimuli. For example, the examiner taps (. ..) and the child is then asked 'Which one of these did you hear?' He is shown three visual arrays to choose from, (...), (. /..) and (.. .). The ability to make such cross-modal or audition-verbal associations has been subjected to some thorough discussion (Beech, 1985) and to some extent the idea has fallen into disrepute. At one stage it was thought that the child with such a problem might be slow to develop the association area of the cortex (in particular the inferior parietal area) (Doehring, 1968; Geschwind, 1964) but again this idea is not as popular as it once was (for full discussion see Downing and Leong, 1983). Nevertheless, the ability to make grapheme-phoneme correspondencies is important. One child seen by the author (Harding, 1983) did not seem to be able to make visual-verbal links. One test, the

Monroe Test (1932) illustrates that this skill was difficult for her. In this children had to learn to associate five nonsense descriptions (e.g. ⌐) with five sounds (e.g. 'Ki'). After three presentations of the sound symbol associations most seven- to eight-year-old children got four out of five correct. Emma was a child who made very confused guesses, getting more right on the third presentation.

More relevantly, her reading was very poor, often consisting of relevant guesses. She read 'John and Ann were fishing' as 'John and Ann were here'. Emma could not use knowledge of phonics or grapheme-phoneme correspondence rules when trying to read new words.

When one suspects such problems it is perhaps wise to carry out some indepth analysis of the specific problems in grapheme-phoneme correspondence. One child might know the single vowels and consonants but have no knowledge of consonantal blends. The Domain Phonics Test, amongst others, can help with such analysis.

<u>Remediation</u>   The usual way that such problems have been remedied is through the child learning a phonics programme as offered by the Domain programme (McLeod and Atkinson, 1972), Alpha and Omega (Hornsby and Shear, 1980), The Stott Programme (1966) and others. Phonics methods have been investigated by Hornsby and Miles (1980) when looking at remedial methods used by specialised schools for backward readers. Naidoo (1981) found that most remedial methods used in schools depended on phonics.

One rather detailed phonics method is that developed by Bradley and Bryant (1983, 1985). This involves the use of plastic alphabet letters. The authors stress that the important part of the method is that the child can see a word being changed whilst certain letters remain the same. For example, removing 'c' from 'cat' gives 'at' which can be changed to 'mat' or 'hat'. The method also gives simultaneous input through sound and vision. It is quite like the methods advised by Maria Montessori in the early part of the century. Her sandpaper letters were used to teach reading and the child could remove letters to make new words. However, the sandpaper letters also provided a certain input from the sense of touch and muscle sense derived from feeling the letters. A combination of these three or four senses - auditory, visual, tactile and kinaesthetic - has long been recognised as an important aspect of remedial reading and is known as the multi-sensory approach. This rests on the assumption that if a child is having difficulty learning one type of association, in this case visual-verbal, then he ought to be able to use different types of association (for example, visual-kinaesthetic and kinaesthetic-verbal) to bridge the gap and help the child to learn.

This type of multi-sensory approach, sometimes called VAKT (visual, auditory, kinaesthetic, tactile), has its roots in the work of Fernald (1921) and Gillingham and Stillman (1956). More recently Hulme (1981) utilised the technique when training retarded readers and normal readers in memory for letters. Specifically, children had to trace over a letter whilst saying it aloud. Gillingham and Stillman's (1956) method involves teaching the words in a specific order and remedial drills. However, the useful multi-sensory part of their work involves all the four senses. The child might be given the word 'milk' to learn for example. The steps would be:

1. 'milk' shown on a card, and   visual
   teacher says 'milk'   visual-auditory

2. child traces 'milk'   visual-tactile/
                                      kinaesthetic

3. child traces 'milk' whilst   auditory-tactile/
                                      kinaesthetic
   the teacher says m-i-l-k   and visual-
                                      kinaesthetic

4. child sees 'milk', traces   visual-tactile/
   'milk' and says 'm-i-l-k   kinaesthetic and
   milk'   auditory-tactile/
                                      kinaesthetic.

In retarded readers memory for letters was increased from 74% to 84% correct by this method (Hulme and Bradley, 1984). A mixture of all modalities, visual, auditory and tactile/kinaesthetic was more effective than training using visual-motor or visual-auditory channels alone by Bradley (1984). The method has been called simultaneous oral spelling by Bradley. Children who used this method increased spelling ability to 58% of words correct, whilst children who received training methods using only visual-motor or visual-auditory channels alone spelt only 30-35% of words correctly. Bradley's work is described in more detail in the section on spelling.

It would seem then that the multi-sensory approach is quite useful in training retarded readers. In particular all senses (apart from smell) need to be used to make the method effective. Presumably this has something to do with bridging the gap between the sight of the word (visual) and its sound (verbal). The reader is referred to Beech (1985) and Bradley and Bryant (1985) for an up-to-date discussion of these methods.

b) Higher-order Language and Conceptualisation

I have already stressed the importance of language skills in relation to reading. Auditory and phonetic skills, as well as a well developed vocabulary, are all important skills. Yet at a higher level the structure of language affects the ability to read. Two American psychologists, Smith and Goodman (1971) put great emphasis on the linguistic aspects of reading. In particular they stress the use of context in learning to read. Poor readers and young readers, it seems, use only graphophonic cues when guessing at unknown words, whereas:

> The more proficient readers are able to read quickly and therefore make more guesses based on context, as they only resort to the surface text for confirmation of their guesses. (Goodman, 1969)

Goodman (1969) has developed an ingenious way for testing the child's use of context and other areas in reading. He analyses the errors or miscues (as he calls them) made by the child along three dimensions. Thus graphophonic, syntactic and semantic similarity measures are distinguished. For graphophonic similarity the miscue must be fairly similar to the original word. For example, the child who reads better as butter would have a fairly high score in this dimension. For syntactic similarity the miscue must have the same grammatical sense as the original word. For example, if the child reads 'John and Ann were playing' as 'John and Ann were running' this would get a fairly high score on the syntactic dimension. For semantic similarity the response given by the child must be similar in meaning to the required response. If the child reads 'the woodman had fallen into the lake' as 'the woodman had fallen into the pond' this would be hardly any change in meaning and the child would obtain a high semantic similarity score.

However it would seem that the use of context is not the major problem for retarded readers that Goodman suggests. Harding (1984) compared the miscues made by a group of children with specific reading disability with those of average readers of the same age and IQ. The disabled readers were very poor at making guesses based on graphophonic knowledge, and therefore had low graphophonic scores. They were similar to the average readers in their use of grammatic cues (syntactic similarity score) and actually better than average readers when it came to the use of context (semantic similarity scores). This research was confirmed by the work of Harding, Beech and Sneddon (1985) when the pattern of miscues for children of reading ages from five to eleven years was mapped. The graphophonic miscue score increased from age five to seven years and then reached a ceiling. The syntactic and semantic similarity scores actually decreased as reading proficiency increased. The opinion that retarded readers are actually poorer at graphophonic word analysis than in the use of context has been reiterated by Bradley and Bryant (1985). They say:

> There is strong evidence that backward readers do depend on context. They use it to help them to work out the meaning of particular words and phrases and they do so at least as much as other children and probably more so.

Nevertheless, it remains an important skill for children to be able to use context and an idea that is popular with teachers. Some researchers, for example Reid (1972), stress the importance of the story-telling register. That is, the child must not only be aware of his own language but the language of books. For children who have little experience of books it may be quite difficult for them to learn to read this new language. Donaldson (1978) makes a similar point when she talks of developing the child's 'reflective awareness' of language. She stresses that children need to be made aware that the language used in speaking is not necessarily the same as that used at school or in books. This awareness is sometimes called meta-linguistic or meta-cognitive awareness, an awareness of the special structure of written text.

Remediation   The general homily that children need to read and be read to must be reiterated at this point. Perhaps it would be useful to go over the various types of register which might assist in developing the child's reflective awareness. Some of these are:

1. Use of rhymes and alliteration. This starts with nursery rhymes and continues into poetry.

2. Folk tales and fairy stories.

3. Modern imaginative stories.

4. Factual texts, starting with labelled photographs, through to the biology text book.

5. Last but not least, the reading primer.

Yet, there is another difficult task for the teacher. He or she needs to present the child with a variety of registers. Yet each must not be too remote from the child's own language otherwise it is alien and the child's attention wanders. Children with little pre-school experience of language have great difficulty in understanding the language of books and primers. This has led to the development of a remedial method known as the language experience approach (Fairman, 1972). In this the child tells his own story to the teacher or gives an account of events in his life which he would like recorded. The teacher writes down this story verbatim and with the help of the child. It is a book which the child can 'read', because the phrases are those that the child uses. The language is then built into the child's next book and new words are added gradually.

In stressing the high order aspects of language such as the use of context, I have referred to Goodman's miscue analysis. A more detailed description of this is given by Goodman (1969). It is sufficient here to say that each of the child's first 25 errors or miscues are analysed in three ways, graphophonic, syntactic and semantic. The child's reading style can then be ascertained and this will give certain remedial recommendations. For example, if a child uses graphophonic cues quite well and context cues less well then the teacher can stress this aspect when he practises reading, asking the child to guess from context.

One method which is used to assist the child in guessing from context is known as the cloze procedure. In the procedure words in the text are deleted and the child's task is to fill in these blanks. Just which words are deleted will be decided by the teacher and she or he may have various aims. For example, the teacher's aim may be i) to make a progression from less difficult to more difficult words, ii) to delete words where various alternatives are appropriate. Degrees of clueing may be given, for example i) the initial letter may be given, ii) a dictionary of possible words is given beneath the text. In using cloze as a teaching technique, however, the deletions should be chosen to promote discussion and develop higher reading skills. The overall method is given by Rye (1982) who suggests that the method is useful if used in conjunction with discussion. Four steps are necessary:

1. The students <u>predict</u> what should fill the gap.
2. They <u>justify</u> their choices.
3. They <u>compare</u> their choices with the original.
4. They <u>comment</u> on the differences.

SUMMARY

With the plethora of research on reading and the enormous
variety of remedial methods which are recommended, it is
quite   difficult   to   make   definitive   statements
recommending specific methods for particular reading
difficulties.
    What   should   be   done   about   Stephen who is eight
years old and can only read a few words? In an ideal
world one might be able to describe accurately his
strengths and weaknesses with a fair degree of accuracy.
Then a specific remedial programme might be designed to
build up the area of weakness and to capitalise on the
strength by attempting to teach him reading through this
channel, as recommended by Johnson and Myklebust (1967).
However, at the present time we do not have the teacher
resources to carry out such an analysis for each child.
    The best compromise for the teacher is for him or
her to make an intelligent guess as to the child's areas
of strength and weakness, based perhaps on observation of
the child's reading with possibly a minimum of testing as
indicated here.   The child might have problems in the
auditory-language area as shown by poor language
development   generally,   difficulty   in   auditory
discrimination, poor speech and so on. For this child it
would be a good idea to teach reading using an
ideo-visual approach (pictures attached to each word) or
the child's own language, thus capitalising on his or her
strengths.   This could be backed up with training in
auditory discrimination and general build up of language.
Training in phonemic awareness, especially coupled with
techniques to illustrate letter-to-sound correspondences,
as advocated by Bradley and Bryant (1985), might also be
useful.   So the child's area of weakness would be built
up.   Later on, as the child became more proficient at
reading, it would be necessary to develop higher order
skills giving training in phonics and higher order
language skills.   So we see that many methods might be
appropriate for one child. The timing of the different
methods is crucial though, as the child needs to
experience some success. The adult literacy classes are
full of people who experienced such early failure,
usually in the form of drilling in phonics which, at that

stage, was meaningless. It is only through a carefully structured one-to-one program and a great deal of motivation on the part of the adult, that such difficulties are overcome.

4. DIFFICULTIES WITH WRITING AND SPELLING

Writing is a complex activity requiring the coordination of several skills. Firstly, the writer has a body of material which he or she wishes to write about. Secondly, he or she has some ability to translate this information into meaningful language. Thirdly, there is appropriate execution of this meaningful language in handwriting. This last aspect, handwriting, is a highly developed skill which the young child executes slowly and with intense concentration. In the adult 'the fine discriminations integrations, memory and coordination of hand, mind and eye required for the act of writing are infinitely complex' (Hughes, 1955).

By the time the child is five or six he or she has developed enough to begin to learn to write. Initially this seems to be a visual-motor activity requiring the accurate copying of name and simple phrases. Gradually, as the child is more and more able to execute letters and words automatically, cognitive and linguistic aspects become important. The child begins to formulate his or her own sentences and phrases. As he or she matures and learns, the written composition becomes increasingly more abstract and phrasing becomes more complex.

Despite a few excellent texts on the subject of writing in recent years (Frith, 1980; Gregg and Steinberg, 1980; Martlew, 1983) our understanding of the nature of learning difficulties in writing and spelling is still at a rudimentary level. It is hardly surprising that there is a dearth of information on the incidence of these learning difficulties. In a survey of learning disabilities, Tansley and Pankhurst (1981) quote an incidence of 5% of children with writing and spelling problems in Germany. The incidence of spelling problems alone was given as 0.4% in New Zealand.

THE CLASSIFICATION OF LEARNING DIFFICULTIES IN WRITING

Writing, Reading and Spelling

Several researchers (Bryant and Bradley, 1980, 1983; Frith, 1980; Read, 1981) have expressed the view that writing is a language skill which is very different from reading. It is not the inverse of reading and probably both have different sources and development. Read (1981) gives the example of his six-year-old daughter who wrote:

Wons a litol grol was wokig in hr gordin until se got kot biy a robr.

Yet the same child could read:

Once a little girl was walking in her garden until she was caught by a robber.

This suggests that the child is utilising two channels of communication or systems of coding, hence Frith's (1980) reference to 'reading by eye and writing by ear'. This distinction has been verified experimentally by Bryant and Bradley (1980) who showed that there were some children who could read words they could not spell and others who could spell words they could not read. In the first category (words read but not spelt) were words such as 'school', 'light', 'train' and 'egg' (from the Schonell Graded Word Spelling Test). These are all irregular words, which would be incorrectly spelt if a phonological code were used. In the second category (words spelt but not read) were words such as 'bun', 'mat', 'leg' and 'pat' (again from the Schonell Test). These are all regular words which can be spelt accurately if a phonological code is used. This suggests that these young children (six-and-a-half-years of age) had different strategies for reading and spelling.

In a further experiment Bryant and Bradley (1983) demonstrate the effect of interference on spelling. Six- and seven-year-old children had to repeat a nonsense syllable ('bla-bla') when trying to write the words depicted on the picture (the child was shown a picture of a cow, for example, and had to write 'cow'). Saying the nonsense syllable reduced the number of words correctly spelt. This suggests that the young children were attempting to use a phonological code in spelling and the saying of a nonsense word interfered with this. The seven-year-olds did not have so much difficulty as the six-year-olds with the easier spellings. The interfering effect of saying 'bla-bla' was not so great. The older children then might have had another spelling route available to them, probably a visual one. So it looks as though the two systems, phonological and visual, fuse as children get older, and that they utilise both in reading and spelling.

The Development of Writing

Young children write mainly for themselves. Read's child did not use the conventions of English spelling. He notes a gradual change from spelling for oneself to the adoption of commonly used forms between ages four to nine years and six to eleven years. It is not until age six (approximately) that there is standardisation of ing endings and abstract generalisations of 'sed' to 'siad' and finally to 'said' and 'ar' to 'aer' to 'are'.

The composition of young writers below age seven (approximately) shows a form of self disclosure. The child writes principally as if he or she were talking. There is little idea of composition or planning. Young children rarely think before they write but rather plunge 'straight in'. There is also little idea of planning or selection of writing for a particular person. The child really writes down everything that comes into her head. An example of a young child's writing is given below:

Writing from Jamie, aged 5 years 6 months.

The dolphin is swimming through the seaweed. There are fish and a crab. A seagull is going to catch fish.

The development of writing is a process which is difficult to trace. But there are some changes which occur over time and have been noted by several researchers. For example, Grumlach (1981) notes an increase in passage length with age. The increase in passage length is also related to the aim of writing. The planning and selection of material though is not seen until the child is 13 or 14 years of age on average according to Stahl (1977), because of the cognitive demands writing makes. Yet, according to Martlew (1983) 10- and 11-year-olds attempt to plan their work. By the age of 11 or 12 years of age most children are showing a difference when attempting to write for adults compared with when attempting to write for children. Some authors, notably Loban (1976) and Bereiter (1980), note a plateau in writing development at about age 13 to 16 years, when writing is quite fluent, but the young writer is not yet able to objectify language and develop a particular writing style. This is thought to be because of the enormous cognitive demands of writing.

Writing, as we have already noticed, requires the integration of many different skills. The writer, in paying attention to these different skills, requires a great cognitive or mental capacity. A pupil must pay attention to handwiriting, word choice, spelling, punctuation, sentence structure and so on. For a young child very few of these skills have become automatic and so it is quite difficult for a child to pay attention to more than one aspect at a time (Scardamelia, 1981).

Bereiter (1980) has developed a five-stage theory of writing development which takes some of these points into account. The first stage, associative writing, is the simplest style, which consists in writing down whatever comes to mind in the order it comes to mind. It is relatively 'unplanned, uninhibited and unconcerned about audience reaction'. This form of writing is one adopted by most junior school children under the age of eight or nine years. Ten-year-olds habitually use it, although they are capable of higher level writing. Associative writing, which is also called expressive writing, is the main form of writing seen in the junior and middle school.

At the next level comes performative writing, which takes into account rules of grammar, spelling, punctuation etcetera. It is the main form of writing, which schooling traditionally attempts to develop. Concern with these aspects often disrupts the flow of writing. Even adults find such aspects disrupting as exemplified by Scardamelia (1981) who quotes an adult as saying, 'I have all my thoughts in my mind but when I come to a word I can't spell it throws me off my writing.'

The third level, communicative writing, develops alongside performative writing. This is when the writer attempts to write for a particular reader. As we have discussed, this occurs only to a very limited extent below the age of 11 or 12 years.

The higher levels of writing are first, unified writing, in which the writer takes account, not only of the reader, but the writer's own perspectives as a writer. It is at this level that the writer begins to objectify language and to be aware of the different forms which might be used. Second, epistemic writing, the final level, is a further development when writing is seen as a personal search for meaning and helps to extend and develop the writer's own thoughts.

So we see the development of writing as a progression from a simple reproductive process to a complex expository style. The children in the junior and middle school are mostly capable of associative writing. Throughout school there is a developing awareness and integration of other aspects of writing, namely the rules of grammar and spelling, the planning of a composition and writing for others.

Myklebust (1967) has described the development of writing as consisting of four levels, which, as they are largely self-explanatory, form a basis for development through junior school and for remediation.

These four levels are:

Concrete - Descriptive

Concrete - Imaginative

Abstract - Descriptive

Abstract - Imaginative

These categories are probably not discrete and may overlap with Bereiter's categories. In particular the two concrete levels are types of associative writing and the two abstract levels are types of unified writing. Although some aspects of writing (namely rules of grammar and spelling) do not form part of this classification, it is useful as a plan for remediation of aspects of composition and will be discussed in greater detail under that heading.

Learning Difficulties in Writing and Spelling

Writing is a complex activity requiring the integration of several different skills. Broadly speaking there are three steps:

(a) Planning and selection of material

(b) Linguistic representation of this material in

    i) sentences and paragraphs
   ii) words (correctly spelt)

(c) Motor execution in handwriting (or typing).

Difficulties in writing may occur in any of these three areas, which are broadly covered in the three types of writing difficulty discussed by Johnson and Myklebust (1967):

(a) Deficiency in formulation (planning and selection, linguistic representation)

(b) Defect in revisualisation (spelling)

75

(c) Disorder of visuo-motor integration (handwriting).

     According to Johnson and Myklebust, these areas of
difficulty are similar to ones seen in adults with brain
damage.   A more recent description of difficulties seen
in adults is given by Marcie (1983) who describes five
areas of deficit in adults. These are:

(a) Agraphia with agrammatical aphasia - a problem with
     syntax construction.

(b) Agraphia with aphasia of phonemic production -
     largely a spelling problem.

(c) Apraxic agraphia - largely a complete loss of
     handwriting movements.

(d) Agraphia with sensory aphasia - understanding of
     words affected.

(e) Pure agraphia - a writing disorder in which defects
     in speech, reading or gestures are affected.

     The last two involve language or the understanding
of language and may overlap with some of the
developmental disorders described in Chapter Two. The
other three may be compared to the three disabilities
described by Johnson and Myklebust.   Agraphia with
agrammatical aphasia is very similar to one aspect of
deficiency in formulation, namely, the problem in
sentence construction. Agraphia with aphasia of phonemic
production is one aspect of a spelling problem (though
perhaps not the one described by Johnson and Myklebust).
Apraxic agraphia may be like the handwriting disorder
seen in children.   However, these comparisons are not
exact and we cannot say that children with these learning
disabilities have any minimal brain damage. Neither the
classification proposed by Johnson and Myklebust or one
based on Marcie's work is sufficient for the
classification of learning difficulties in writing and
spelling seen in children.   I would propose a more
comprehensive classification as set out below.

Figure 4.1:   Proposed Classification of Learning
Difficulties in Writing and Spelling

     Writing difficulties

     a) Difficulties in composition

                Formulation and planning
                Grammatical structure
    b)   Difficulties with handwriting

    Spelling and other difficulties

    a)   Spelling difficulties
    b)   Problems with punctuation and spacing

WRITING DIFFICULTIES

a) Difficulties in Composition

In the discussion of the development of writing it became
apparent that much of what we call writing is actually a
cognitive task.   The planning and selection of material
and the formulation of ideas in composition is one major
aspect of this. The second aspect is the translation of
this material into a grammatically constructed form.
These will be considered in turn.

Difficulty in Formulation and Planning In thinking of
the junior school child it must be realised that very few
children will be attempting to write for others in any
meaningful way.   The coordination of planning, sentence
structure and spelling at the end of the performative
writing stage will be very difficult. Most children will
be attempting to do this, however, and much of the
teaching at junior school will be directed towards
producing such integrated composition.
        Learning difficulties in this area may not be
apparent until the child is eight or nine years of age as
in the first two years of schooling the child is required
to write little more than single, simple sentences. It
is at the point where children are beginning to write
stories and letters that such difficulties are revealed.
Very often the difficulties are due to a basic language
difficulty as a child cannot write without the basis of a
good vocabulary, good language facility and good general
knowledge.   Johnson and Myklebust (1967) believe that
there are children who have good oral language, can read
well and can copy well, but cannot express their ideas in
writing. This is thought to be because the child is able
to convert thoughts to some forms of expression (verbal
or in drawing) but not others (written). Myklebust's
(1967) Picture Story Language Test is supposed to reveal
the discrepancy between oral and written language.

Remediation   Myklebust's (1967) classification of the

levels of creative writing mentioned earlier can form a good basis for ideas about remediation. Any child who has limited written expression in the primary school will be at the concrete - descriptive level. Initially the first requirement will be for the child to write very simple sentences (e.g. 'This is my dog. He is in his basket.') which are purely written verbalisation. The child should then be encouraged to develop more imaginative expression. For example, Johnson and Myklebust (1967) suggest that the teacher should select an object and ask the child to think of as many ways of describing it as possible (e.g. 'a big, blue ball'). A similar activity is suggested in Kirk's Illinois Test of Psycholinguistic Abilities. The child is given an object and asked to describe it along several dimensions in answer to questions. For example, the following might be asked: 'What colour is it?' 'What size is it?' 'What shape is it?' 'What do you use it for?' If the object is a button, the child might answer: 'red, big, round, for fastening my coat'. Much of this type of activity can be performed verbally at first and then later the child can be encouraged to write the phrases down.

Simple sentences are then introduced. Typically this is achieved with the use of pictures. Tough (1976) has produced a series of these to assist with language development in the infant school but they might also be used at a later stage to assist in writing. At this level the child should be persuaded to write a sequence of activities in answer to questions such as: 'What is the little boy doing?' 'What do you think will happen next?' 'How will the little boy feel about that?'

These activities are all at the concrete - imaginative level, though with the introduction of ideas regarding previous and future events and feelings an element of abstraction is introduced. The child must infer ideas from the pictures or experience. To teach such inference Johnson and Myklebust (1967) suggest that we start with fairly concrete experiences familiar to all children. For example, we might start with a boy eating and the child has to imagine what he is eating, or a little girl getting dressed and the child has to imagine where she is going.

Further developments at the abstract - descriptive level involve the sequencing of events in a story. The ideal activity for this is to provide the child with pictures which can be sequenced in a kind of strip cartoon. The sequences can be short (about three pictures) and depict a very simple story to begin with. Gradually more complicated sequences and events are introduced. Learning Development Aids supply sets of such pictures in their picture sequencing cards which can be used by individual children for language and writing development. The keeping of a diary or the sequencing of events in the day or the week are useful activities too. At the upper end of the abstract - descriptive level the child should try to present different characters. Play activities and the writing of plays are useful for this.

The last level of written work, the abstract - imaginative, is one that few junior school children will be capable of to any great extent. Stories should consist of imaginative setting, sequenced plot and a story with an adequate (possibly moralistic) conclusion. The teacher can guide thinking with appropriate discussion and questioning to assist the production of mature text. (See Johnson and Myklebust, 1967; Weber, 1978 for suggestions.)

Difficulties with Grammatical Structure   The second requirement of a piece of writing is that it should be presented in adequately formed sentences and paragraphs. Of course, written English can be analysed into parts of speech, subject and object, noun, verb, adjective and so on. But no child with a learning difficulty is going to benefit from such analysis.

Remediation   The first requirement for a child who is going to write adequately is that his or her oral language be both clear and interesting. The child with poor oral language is hardly going to be able to write well. The reader is referred to Chapter Two for discussion on remediation of this problem. Assuming the child's oral expression is fair, the child must be encouraged to transfer this language to writing. One useful way to do this is to use his oral language to develop his own book (see Chapter Three). This has been used as a way of teaching reading (Fairman, 1972) but it can be used as a method of teaching writing. The teacher will of course need to modify the text slightly towards good grammatical structure.

A similar technique is advised by Giordano (1983). He thinks there is a considerable overlap between speech and writing and that teachers should use language skills in speech to develop writing. Remediation should begin with children's spontaneously uttered and then written passages. This is called the communicative writing sample and should be of interest to the child, for example, a dream. In order to develop grammatical structure, words in the text are deleted and then restored. In the restoration phase pupils have to rewrite the passage. Because they are concentrating on

the words to be restored they are less likely to
duplicate the errors made in the original passage. Any
remaining errors can be discussed at a later stage. This
reminds us of the cloze technique advocated by Rye (1982)
to develop grammatical awareness in reading. But it can
be used to develop writing.

Figure 4.2:   Example of remedial exercises undertaken
with a communicative writing sample (Giordano, 1983)

---

1. Communicative writing sample
    Harry started the fight.   He did it because John
    wasn't wrong. It was his cards. He didn't even have
    to share. And Billy wished so and agreed to. So you
    saw Harry did it the time like he stoled the prize.

2. Words deleted
    ..... started the fight.   He did it because John
    wasn't ...... It was his ...... He didn't even have
    to share. And Billy .... agreed to. So you
    saw Harry did it the time like he ...... the prize.

3. Restoration phase
    Harry started the fight.   He did it because John
    wasn't wrong. They were his cards. He didn't even
    have to share and Billy agreed to. So you saw Harry
    did it the time like he stole the prize.

4. Discussion phase
    So you saw Harry etc....

Giordano has also suggested the following exercises:

1. Delete ends of sentences on worksheets
    e.g. Darkness
         Darkness makes me feel ....
         Something that might be hidden darkness
         is........
         If I were in a dark place without light I would
         ....

2. Have picture stories with words erased from balloons.

        Johnson and Myklebust (1967) have also suggested
various exercises.   In one such example a picture is
selected and several phrases or sentences are written
underneath.   The child has to pick the correct one.   The
sentence choices can be graded in difficulty, an easy and
a difficult choice being given below. Initially the

child is encouraged to read the sentences orally several times or discuss it with a friend to get the correct choice. Later the child will be expected to make his choice without verbalisation. Such an exercise can be adapted into a form of lotto.

Easy choice	Difficult choice
The girls is skated.	The boys is fishing.
The girls are skating.	The boys am fishing
The girls am skated.	The boys are fishing.

b) Difficulties with Handwriting

A further aspect of writing is its execution in handwriting. From the first stumbling copying of the child's name to the flowing style of the adult, there is a gradual development of automaticity. The act of writing requires less conscious effort and becomes a precise skill. Luria (1973) has described the development of this skill as a functional development of various parts of the brain. He refers to the kinetic melody of handwriting as the functional integration of hand, the sensory and motor parts of the brain controlling movement, the eye and visual cortex, the language areas and the association areas, and the frontal cortex (the thinking part). The degree of involvement of the different parts in this most complex activity varies according to the age and stage of the child.

Johnson and Myklebust (1967) describe disorders of handwriting as occurring in a child who has neither a visual nor a motor defect. The defect is in visual-motor integration. In other words, they see the child with a handwriting disability as one who has difficulty in translating visual information to the motor activity. There is little evidence regarding the nature of handwriting difficulties, but I would assume that a disability in visual-motor integration is not the only source of difficulty.

Writing disability can occur with or without reading difficulty or other language problems. Orton (1937) comments 'a developmental agraphia might coexist with a reading and spelling disability, but a writing disability is encountered not infrequently as an isolated disorder'.

The writing disability can be seen in several degrees. At the most severe, the child cannot copy the simplest of designs. Others can reproduce writing (copy) but the sequence of movements is entirely meaningless to him or her and they cannot write their own words.

Ellis (1982) thinks that children with writing

problems or developmental dysgraphia are really no different from normal children and adults who also have 'slips of the pen'. Their problems are only perhaps more severe, but no different in kind. Ellis classifies the various types of writing error as follows:

(a) Reversals, e.g. 'gosd' for 'gods'.

(b) Orientation errors, e.g. 'bogs' for 'dogs'. (This occurs with letters 'pq', 'nm', 'ao', 'rv', 'hk', 'db'.)

(c) Contaminations - the fusion of two adjacent letters which is seen in adults when writing quickly and slovenly, e.g. ⌣ for 'ing', (⌐ for 'from'.

We might also add the following from the work of Peters (1967).

(d) Other forms of contractions, e.g. 'kiten' for 'kitten', 'telesion' for 'television'.

(e) Perseverations, e.g. 'bananana' for 'banana'.

Remediation   Johnson and Myklebust (1967) stress that careful observation of the particular child's difficulties is necessary before correct remediation can be carried out. It would be useful to observe the extent to which a child can copy the types of movement made, whether the child watches his hand as he writes, whether he verbalises as he writes and so on.

If the child's disability is very severe he may need to engage in a variety of prewriting activities as suggested by Johnson and Myklebust (1967), Kephart (1971) and Frostig and Maslow (1973). Broadly speaking these activities should involve the integration of visual, auditory, kinaesthetic and tactile senses. In prewriting activities, for example the drawing of a circle, the child follows a pattern by touch or muscle sense. This is achieved initially by the child following a pattern with his finger (felt, sandpaper and clay pan patterns are suitable, as well as making large patterns in the air), getting kinaesthetic and tactile feedback. The child may in addition verbalise (e.g. around), obtaining auditory feedback and of course, in observing his movements, visual feedback is obtained. A variety of stencils can be given to provide more difficult feedback, two examples being given below. Tracing, copying and blackboard work are more difficult still. Another general principle to observe is the development from

large to small patterns, transferring from gross to fine
movements. Also the direction of movement should be in
accordance with the flow used in writing. The child
should be encouraged to make the movement in one piece.

Simple stencil for O   Difficult stencil for O

 = card

   These same principles can be observed in the
teaching of writing or printing in accordance with the
VAKT technique pioneered by Gillingham and Stillman
(1956). This technique is discussed further in the
section on spelling, but simple printed letters can be
taught by use of felt or 3D letters, blackboard,
dot-to-dot tracing etcetera. It is interesting to note
that this method has been used in the past to teach
handwriting to five- and six-year-olds (Montessori, 1945;
Froebel, 1912). Writing patterns can also encourage the
development of the flow of writing and automaticity.
   This brings us to one controversial issue which is
relevant to remedial and the initial teaching of
handwriting. This is the question of whether to teach
manuscript or cursive handwriting. Manuscript writing
involves the writing of letters separately (or printing),
whereas cursive handwriting is a flowing style. The
teaching of manuscript letters is advocated by some (e.g.
Johnson and Myklebust, 1967) largely because the
movements are simpler than those in cursive writing and
there are fewer changes in letter forms. For example,
the 'o' in 'on' is different from the 'o' in 'no' in
cursive writing. In addition the form of manuscript
writing is much closer to the script seen in reading
books. However others, including Strauss and Lehtinen
(1947), argue that children with learning disabilities
should be taught cursive handwriting, because the rhythm
involved in cursive handwriting lends itself to the
production of automatic skilled movements. It is also
argued that cursive writing helps to hold words together
in units and, as such, there will be few transposition

errors (e.g. 'gril' for 'girl') (Byers, 1963).

In an American study, Early, Nelson, Kleber, Treegoob, Huffman and Cass (1976) compared five-year-old children who had been taught cursive writing with those who had been taught manuscript (cursive handwriting is the style which is taught predominantly in schools in the USA). Though there was no significant difference in IQ between the groups at the beginning of the year, by the end of the year the children who had been taught cursive writing were superior in the Stanford Word Reading and Spelling Tests and showed fewer reversal and transposition errors in writing. However, we should note that this study was not carried out with learning disabled children. In this country forms of manuscript writing (e.g. Marion Richardson, Italic) are commonly taught and this fact might persuade us in favour of manuscript writing. The most important factor, however, is that of consistency. The child should be taught a particular type thoroughly.

Another factor which might affect handwriting is the use of lined or unlined paper. In a study by Lindsay and McLennan (1984) children below the age of six years were found to produce more legible writing when they used unlined paper. In addition the work on unlined paper was judged creatively better than the work on lined paper by two independent judges for these six-year-olds. With children aged seven years and older, however, the reverse was true. The more legible and creative writing was produced on lined paper. With learning-disabled children of eight or nine years we might assume that their handwriting might be developmentally at the six-year-old level and if this is the case unlined paper would be preferable. This would require confirmation by adequate research however.

SPELLING AND OTHER DIFFICULTIES

Spelling difficulties

Spelling and reading have different roots in development, as discussed earlier through the work of Bradley and Bryant (1983, 1985), Frith (1980) and Read (1981). Initially spelling is a phonological skill and reading a visual one primarily. Normally, by the age of seven or eight years these visual and phonological elements become fused and the child uses both processes.

It is hardly surprising therefore that it is at this age that spelling difficulties are first noticed. In the mature speller, spelling is a three-stage process (as described by Frith, 1980). It involves the correct analysis of speech sounds, the conversion of phonemes to graphemes and, thirdly, a visual check that spelling is correct. One might also add a further element, an aspect stressed by Johnson and Myklebust (1967) in the writing of graphemes. For example, a child may know how a word is spelt (TRAIN) and can visualise it in his head, but he might be unable to write the word correctly. So we can say that there are four steps in the spelling process.

i) Analysis of speech sounds (saying or sounding in head, otherwise called oral spelling).

ii) Conversion of phonemes to graphemes.

iii) Writing of graphemes.

iv) Visual check.

Ellis (1982), however, says there are two routes commonly used by the mature speller, only one of which is that described above. A mature speller normally uses a vocabulary or lexicon of whole words with which he or she is very familiar. The word is written as a whole, the writer having an entire kinetic memory for the word. When an adult is writing he or she very rarely spells or sounds out a word, though, of course, this route can be used with an unfamiliar word. Writing and spelling are mainly automatic skills. So we have two routes to spelling in the mature speller, the normally preferred lexical route and the phoneme-grapheme route which can be used with unfamiliar words.

Thus a child with difficulties in spelling may have a problem with any of the several processes described above. Nelson and Warrington (1974) describe two types of spelling-disabled child. Those who have a reading and spelling difficulty combined and those who have only a spelling difficulty. Children with a spelling problem alone tended to have difficulty in visualising the word. In this case the visual lexicon was a problem area and usually the errors made were phonetically accurate (e.g. the child might spell 'yacht' as 'yot'). Children with a reading and spelling difficulty tended to have an underlying language problem and made both visual and phonological errors. Boder (1973) also describes two main types of reading/spelling-disabled child. The first type, the dyseidetic dyslexic, has a visual problem and attempts to write words phonetically. So he or she might write 'stah' for 'star', 'hows' for 'house', 'muthr' for 'mother'. The second type, the dysphonetic dyslexic, makes errors which are similar to the original word visually, but bear no phonetic resemblance (e.g. 'class' for 'star', 'loose' for 'house', 'wutter' for 'mother'). The first type, the dyseidetic dyslexic, is obviously attempting to use the phoneme-grapheme conversion route, where the second type, the dysphonetic dyslexic, is attempting to use the lexical route.

Although we can differentiate these two types of spelling difficulty, many children show errors of both kinds and it would be difficult to classify them as having one difficulty or another. Bryant and Bradley (1983) demonstrate that children use both these systems when spelling but they may not recognise when it is appropriate to use them. They quote the case of Tony, an 11-year-old boy who is at the eight-year-old level as regards reading and spelling, though he is good at mathematics. He is capable of using the phomeme-grapheme conversion route in spelling as he can write out nonsense words such as 'pring', 'blim' etcetera. He is also capable of using the visual route by writing irregularly spelt words correctly (e.g. 'shepherd', 'trouser'). One anomaly was that he could write went and down, but not 'bent' (spelt 'bedet') and 'frown' (spelt 'fran'). This is due to his using the visual route when writing 'went' and 'down', but being unable to make the analogy from these words to 'bent' and 'frown'. He also failed to use the phoneme-grapheme route when writing them. Bryant and Bradley conclude, 'we think the failure to use his memory to make the word "bent" was due to his not recognising that there was a chance to use his existing phonological skills'. So we can recognise that a child's spelling difficulties may occur because of an inability to use the two routes available, or a failure to recognise that different routes can be used, or both.

Remediation   Broadly speaking the remedial techniques advocated for spelling difficulties fall in with the two types of difficulty described. Firstly there are those concerned with improving visual and kinaesthetic memory for the whole word and, secondly, those aimed at improving phoneme-grapheme conversion.
Johnson and Myklebust (1967) advise that difficulties with revisualisation be dealt with as follows. Recall exercises should be given where the child is given part of a word and has to recall the whole word or make the word into a kind of sum. An example of these are given below:

a.   Circle the correct spelling.

```
please      pencil      littel

plaez       pensil      little
```

b. Supply the missing letters.

```
               pen ___

               break ___

               ___ day

               tele ___
```

c. Supply the missing letters.

```
        cat        laugh

        c_t        la_gh

        ca_        laug_

        _at        _ugh
```

d. Find the word on the right which is the same as that on the left.

```
        train / trian, raint, trani, train
```

As mentioned earlier, the VAKT methods of Fernald (1943) and Gillingham and Stillman (1956), utilising all the senses, have also been used to improve spelling. Recently, Hulme (1981) has used this technique and has demonstrated that writing out a word or variants of a word can help a child decide a correct spelling pattern. Although his work was mainly with normal readers, he demonstrated that tracing round letters with the index finger improved memory for letters and words in retarded readers.   The child had to take incorrectly spelt words and either trace over the felt or 3-dimensional letters which spell the word. Thus the child has simultaneous visual and tactile feedback.   The visual memory for poorly spelt words was significantly improved in retarded readers (though not normal readers) by the use of this method.
The second type of difficulty involving the phoneme-grapheme conversion route is stressed by most remedial specialists. The exercises advocated by Johnson and Myklebust (1967) mostly fell into this category, as

does any technique which stresses phonics and word lists. For example, Peters (1970) advocates teaching a child to spell using words from his or her own word list. Those words commonly used in the child's own free writing. Peters demonstrated that using the child's own words produced greater improvement than using published word lists. The strategy advocated for teaching spelling was for the child to be shown the word, then subvocalise the spelling and then to write it.

Lehr (1984) also stresses that the child's own words should be used to teach spelling. Any rules should be taught one at a time when the child is ready for them (when he or she is cognitively advanced enough to understand them). With reference to word lists, Lehr would advise that some can be useful. There is some advantage in teaching the most frequently used words since 2,800 to 3,000 words account for 90% of all the words most people use in a lifetime, and 100 words account for 50% of the words all children use.

Ganschow (1984) recommends that we not only take the spelling list for the child's own work, but that we analyse the errors made and use this as a basis for remediation. She gives the example of Jay, who has only 50% of his words spelt correctly. The errors are analysed by using a table of four columns, as given below:

Mistake	Correct word	Kind of mistake	Remediation
wut	what	Common rule for irregular word	Learn irregular spellings
mas	makes	Sound omission	Sounding out technique
wus	was	Common rule for irregular word	Learn irregular spellings
hast	home	Non-phonetic	Teach sounds
scrd	scared	Vowel omission	Sounding out. Teach words, vowels (cat, cot, cut)

In general this analysis showed that the child had not grasped rudimentary sound-symbol correspondence rules. So remediation should begin with regular patterns of three letter words, and the use of the sounding out technique. Irregularly spelt words should be taught separately.

Some commercially produced materials can be of use in conjunction with this, for example Alpha to Omega

(Hornsby and Shear, 1980) the Domain Phonics Test Kit and Programme (McLeod and Atkinson, 1972), the Stott programme (Stott, 1966) and several materials from Learning Development Aids can be used.

The natural rhythm of a word can be taught by the use of rhymes. For example the kind of exercises where children have to supply words that rhyme, e.g. 'Give me a word that rhymes with pot', 'I need a word to finish this rhyme'. Alliteration can also be taught in this way. 'Today's sound is M. Mary, Mary made a mad...'.

For other children movement can assist with the teaching of this rhythm. I remember learning several spellings from an English teacher who insisted on accompanying arm swinging and shooting movements for certain words spelt orally. The words 'rhythm' and 'necessary' involved, respectively, two and three swings of the arm. Accommodation was a swinger and doubler, spelt 'a, double c, o double m, o, dat, ion. There is no doubt that these spellings are firmly imprinted on my oral memory.

With the exception of Hulme's (1981) study, these recommendations for the teaching of spelling do not provide us with any evidence as to whether one type of remedial method is better or worse than any other. The methods may be of interest to the remedial teacher but in the main the methods are applied to all children. What is needed are studies where some children are taught by the specified technique and others receive some other forms of instruction. One of the few studies of this type which have been carried out is that of Bradley (1981). This work will be considered in some detail as it does provide some evidence regarding the effectiveness of a particular remedial technique.

The remedial technique advocated by Bradley is that of simultaneous oral spelling. The technique is broadly similar to Gillingham and Stillman's (1956) method but Bradley used words for the children's own vocabularies, whereas Gillingham and Stillman advocate lengthy particular sounds in sequence. The method can be described in five steps:

1. The student proposes the word he wants to learn.
2. The word is written correctly for him (or made with plastic letters).
3. The student names the word.
4. He then writes the word himself, saying the alphabetic name of each letter of the word as it is written (copy).
5. He names the word again and checks that it is written correctly.

This sequence is repeated two to five times more with the student covering or disregarding the structure word as soon as he feels he can do without it. The procedure takes about 30 seconds per word and uses visual, auditory and kinaesthetic senses. In Bradley's main experiment 36 eleven-year-old children who were poor spellers were taught by one of four methods. One group received simultaneous oral spelling (SOS), as described above. The second group, visual-auditory-motor (VAM), was taught in a similar way but was not taught to sound out individual letters. A third group had the motor element omitted as they did not write out the word (VA) and a fourth group was untaught. The children were taught four words by one method one day and on other days were taught four other words by use of the other methods, so the experiment observed proper controls. The words taught were: 'sew, buy, toe, won, calf, suit, ache, sign, tyre, tear, soup, cute, laugh, tough, chief, juice', and were all incorrectly spelt by each of the children at the beginning of the experiment. The children were tested for their spelling of the words on three different occasions, the first one day after having been taught it, the second two weeks later and the third four weeks later. Although the three methods produced similar results on the first post-test, SOS proved to be the superior method two weeks and four weeks later. Bradley concludes that 'simultaneous oral spelling is effective because it promotes the organisation of the correct writing pattern'. She stresses that the word must be organised before the child can learn to spell correctly.

Spelling Reform   One approach to help children to learn to read and spell more easily is to reform the irregular English spelling system. Spelling reform has taken place in many countries with the result that most languages are much more regular in spelling. The major problem of irregular spelling is that it makes phonics teaching much more difficult because there are frequent violations of the relationship between particular letters or letter combinations and their corresponding sounds. The impediment to the beginning reader is illustrated by how much more easily children on regularly spelled reading schemes (e.g. ita) reach acceptable standards of reading. Unfortunately they fall back to the normal levels when they have to transfer inevitably over to normal spelling. One obvious difficulty is that it would be expensive to change over to a new spelling scheme; however, most reading materials that are read are produced in the short-term (e.g. newspapers, magazines, memos and so on) so reform for most material could be achieved quickly. Another difficulty is that adults would find it difficult to cope with a new scheme. But this may also be countered, because reading comprehension and speed soon reverts to normal in adults if the reform is sufficiently mild (about 3 in 10 words changed), according to experimental evidence (Beech, 1983). Other reasons against change are that first, different spellings of the same word (e.g. 'be', 'bee') preserve different meanings, and second, that one can see the origins of the word if the original foreign spelling is preserved. These last reasons are not convincing. We can differentiate meanings by context, otherwise we could not understand spoken language and as far as preserving the sources of words is concerned, surely this is far less important than getting children to read?

Having covered these arguments for reform, it is unlikely to take place as it would prove too damaging to whichever political party attempted it. The Americans achieved a mild spelling reform at the beginning of the century and spelling reform did achieve a positive vote in parliament in the forties in the United Kingdom. However, the government of the day diverted the bill by proposing what became the ita experiment. On both sides of the Atlantic the move for spelling reform has died down and all that is left is the relatively small but enthusiastic Simplified Spelling Society.

SUMMARY

Although this chapter is entitled 'Difficulties with Writing and Spelling' the topic covers difficulties at many different levels. The various skills involved in what appears to be a simple act from conceptualisation to motor execution have been discussed at length. Even though the difficulties were discussed under four main headings all of these areas need to be intact to produce a reasonable piece of written text.

A child may have difficulty in just one of these areas, several or all of them. When a child's writing is so obviously poor that many difficulties are apparent it seems unlikely that he will be motivated to write in the long term. The approach then becomes one of the teaching of writing for meaningful purposes, the writing of brief notes or letters and the writing of shopping lists and memory aids. However, this opens the question of whether children with learning disabilities should receive the impoverished education that is implied by such a proposal or whether all educational avenues should be offered to him. This issue has received some attention with reference to the curriculum for the lower streams in schools by Bantock (1980), Peters (1967) etcetera. Whilst this issue may be of theoretical interest, I suspect that the practicalities of teaching learning-disabled children means that all avenues are not offered to them.

5. VISUAL-MOTOR PROBLEMS AND ACTIVITY LEVEL

Over the last twenty or thirty years difficulties in this area have received much attention. It has increasingly been recognised that difficulties in visual perception and problems in coordination and movement can affect learning in the classroom. The work of Kephart (1970) and Frostig and Maslow (1973) with respect to visual perceptual problems has been of much value. In addition there is an increasing interest in children with more severe handicaps either with gross motor difficulties (clumsy children) or with problems in attention and activity level (hyperactivity).

As these problems are only just being recognised there is some uncertainty as to the numbers of children involved. Estimates of numbers of clumsy children vary between 5% and 8% (Dawdy, 1981). This seems to be a reasonably accurate estimate as Gubbay (1975), in a large survey of 997 Australian children, found 5.7% were clumsy. This figure is confirmed by Henderson and Hall (1982) who found 5% of 200 children surveyed in the south of England were clumsy.

Estimates of the incidence of hyperactivity show less uniformity. Shaffer, McNamara and Pincus (1974) quote wide ranging estimates. For example, in the USA Lapouse and Monk (1958) found more than 50% of mothers rated their sons as hyperactive. In the Isle of Wight study Rutter, Tizard and Whitmore (1970) found that 35% of boys were thought to be abnormally restless by their parents when only 16% were thought to be restless by their teachers. There is considerable variation in the estimates of hyperactivity given in clinic populations. In the USA Greenberg and Lipman (1971) found 40% of children seen in clinics had been diagnosed as hyperactive, though in England only 1.6% of such children have been judged as being hyperactive (Rutter et al, 1970). Ross and Ross (1976) reported that 2% of elementary school children in the USA are receiving medication for hyperactivity.

Estimates of the numbers of children with visual perception difficulties are more difficult as it is almost impossible to test visual skills by themselves. There is almost always a motor component. Visual perceptual difficulties are usually associated with motor

93

difficulties. Hulme, Smart and Moran (1982) found a correlation of 0.62 between tests of the two abilities.

LEARNING DIFFICULTIES IN THE VISUAL-MOTOR AREA

One problem with designating a child as hyperactive or clumsy or a child with a perceptual problem is that of heterogeneity. These subcategories are by no means discrete. A clumsy child, for example, besides having gross motor problems, has many other learning difficulties. He or she may be hyperactive and is quite likely to have difficulties with reading and/or writing. This problem of overlap between learning difficulties was discussed in Chapter One. We can recognise that a child may have a learning difficulty in more than one area. It is useful to think of each learning difficulty as discrete without labelling the child. We can think of the child as having a learning difficulty in motor coordination (and perhaps reading and writing) without labelling him as a clumsy child. Thinking of the learning difficulties a child may have is useful as it helps us to pinpoint his or her specific needs, which is the first step on the way to remediation.

A way of classifying the learning difficulties which will be used in the rest of the chapter and which occurs in the visual-motor area is offered below:

Figure 5.1: Provisional classification of learning difficulties in the visual-motor area.

Visual-motor difficulties
    a) visual perceptual difficulties
    b) motor difficulties (clumsiness)

Difficulty with attention and activity level (Hyperactivity)

VISUAL-MOTOR DIFFICULTIES

a) <u>Visual-perceptual difficulties.</u>

Brenner, Gillman, Zangwill and Farrell (1967), in a survey of 810 school children aged between eight and nine years, found a very high percentage (6.7%) exhibited visual-motor learning difficulties. This would seem to be a very high percentage of children. Presumably such learning difficulties would affect attainment in all sorts of areas, but visual perceptual difficulties have been largely unrecognised in this country. The picture in the USA is somewhat different with psychologists such as Frostig and Maslow (1973) and Kephart (1970) devising extensive training programmes in the area.

Frostig, Lefener and Whittlesey (1966) went so far as to develop a test of visual perceptual skills which she claimed is an important precursor of learning to read. Any child who had a perceptual quotient of 90 at six years of age was unlikely to be ready to learn to read (Frostig and Maslow, 1973). However, this claim is not supported by the evidence. Wedell (1968) also claimed that perceptual-motor development is largely a question of motivation.

<u>Remediation</u> Training in visual-motor skills may have some degree of success. There are different approaches to training skills. Both the Frostig and Horne (1973) and Kephart (1970) approaches emphasise fine motor skills. The Frostig and Horne (1973) battery emphasises five areas which are visual-motor coordination, figure-ground, perceptual constancy, position in space and spatial relationships. Whilst these areas may not represent discrete abilities, training in them could be useful. To give one example: position in space is the ability to discriminate position and to differentiate letters such as 'd' and 'b', 'w' and 'm', 'n' and 'u', and words such as 'was/saw'. In the test children have to find the form which is rotated, or find the form which is like the first one in a row, as given in the examples below:

1. Find the form that is reversed or rotated.

2. Find the form like the first one.

Frostig suggests that many exercises, besides paper and pencil ones, can help to develop this skill. For example, the child could be trained in body awareness by copying various positions. Other examples include training in finding and drawing mirror images and 'Simon says'... exercises when Simon says such things as 'move your right leg'. The National Council for Special Education has also published a leaflet of suggested exercises.

Kephart's (1970) work is rather more extensive as he emphasised gross motor and fine motor skill development. In the context of perceptual-motor development his ideas on the development of the perceptual-motor match are highly relevant. He believed that 'the child uses his motor response to the environment for the purpose of attaching meaning to the incoming perceptual information'. For the young child the visual stimulus does not correspond to the feedback from the motor area, creating a mismatch (e.g. the feel of a square object does not correspond to the visual impression which may be a ▱). By careful graded activities the child's visual image could be made to match the motor feedback so that, at first, the eye follows the hand, later the hand follows the eye. On the blackboard, the child would be encouraged to make large movements, first in terms of a general scribble, and then in terms of large round movements, the eye following the hand in all cases. Later, a definite form would be imposed, for example, a circle, but often a template would be used for the initial teaching of this.

The assumption behind all these training procedures which have an extensive and detailed literature, is that such motor exercises will directly feed back and implant themselves, or program, the child's visual perceptual skills.

b) Motor difficulties (clumsiness)

Motor difficulties occurring in childhood have been recognised for some time and were usually called developmental apraxia and developmental agnosia (Gubbay, 1975). The term 'clumsy child' was first used by Walton, Ellis and Court (1962) to describe five children who had problems with motor coordination and skilled motor activity. The syndrome was thought to be a type of minimal cerebral palsy. In this initial study the children showed difficulty with voluntary movements (such as kicking balls) but also involuntary movements occurred (such as fidgeting). They found deficits occurring in everyday activities such as dressing, feeding and walking, and in academic activities such as writing, drawing and copying (see Figure 5.2). Most children exhibited crossed laterality, mixed handedness, and had problems with body image. They mostly had higher verbal IQs than performance IQs.

Figure 5.2:   Attempts at drawing by a clumsy child aged 10 years 6 months.

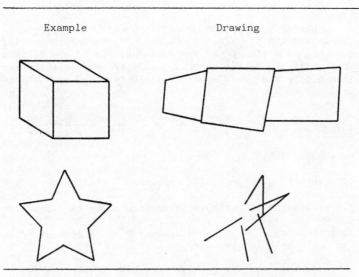

Example   Drawing

Whilst the term 'clumsy child' is attractive and helps us to conjure a picture of the child, it is inexact in that most children who have problems in the visuo-motor area also have difficulties in other areas. Not only is there clumsiness in everyday activities, but problems with handwriting, drawing and speech are common and often the child is highly distractable (Dawdy, 1981). Hulme, Biggerstaff, Moran and McKinlay (1982) have also reviewed visual and kinaesthetic perception in these children.   They found a correlation of 0.62 between visual and perception tests in clumsy children. The motor problem can occur in isolation also, as in the child who 'cannot make his hands do what his eyes see' (Wedell, 1972). Henderson and Hall (1982) also point to the heterogeneity of symptoms including problems with speech, social perception, drawing and reading.   In their study of the sixteen children who had been identified as clumsy, nine had speech or hearing problems, seven showed social immaturity and eight were poor at reading. The incidence of these learning difficulties was not in an ordinary group of children, i.e. those who were not clumsy.   The term 'motor difficulty' might be preferable to 'clumsy children' as it allows a child to have other learning difficulties.   The term 'clumsy child' implies that this is the only learning difficulty in the child.

The motor difficulties shown by these children are in three main areas. There are difficulties with everyday activities (eating, dressing and so on), difficulties with gross motor activity and difficulties with fine motor activity.

Gubbay (1975) has conducted a large survey of children with these difficulties. The 992 children were screened as clumsy by their performance on eight tests which mainly reflect gross and fine motor activities, though only one is an everyday activity. The eight tests are listed below:

Test items for screening clumsy children (after Gubbay, 1975)

Fine motor activity

1.   Whistling.

2.   Threading 10 beads in 38 seconds.

3.   Piercing 20 holes in graph paper in 24 seconds (i.e. each hole in 1mm square).

4.   Posting all objects in a Kiddicraft posting box in 18 seconds.

5.   Tying shoe laces in a double bow in 15 seconds.

Gross motor activity

6.   Five skips with a skipping rope.

7.   Rolling a tennis ball round matchboxes in 18 seconds.

8.   Throwing up a tennis ball, clapping hands four times, and catching it.

Children below the age of eight years were allowed to fail six of these tests without being labelled clumsy, but 12-year-olds were only allowed to fail two. Parents of a child who was identified as clumsy in this test reported that the child was poor at sport, and was slow to learn such activities as blowing the nose, catching a ball and getting dressed for school.

Other tests which can help to assess such motor problems in children are the Bender-Gestalt, the Draw-a-Man Test, the Stott Motor Impairment Test (Stott, Moyes and Henderson, 1972) and items from various child screening tests such as the Croydon Check List. Although such tests can be useful for screening purposes, clumsiness or motor incoordination is more usefully observed in everyday activities. For example, the ten-year-old child who invariably buttons his coat incorrectly, falls over objects, trips whilst going upstairs, is a messy eater and writes unintelligibly, would be thought of as having severe learning difficulties in the motor area. It is likely that motor difficulties are found in different areas as the child gets older. The young child is most likely to have problems with dressing and movement around the classroom. The older child is more likely to demonstrate problems in fine motor activities such as drawing and writing, though difficulties may also be apparent in sport and creative subjects such as art, pottery, cookery and woodwork. Children who do have such difficulties may go unrecognised and can be labelled as lazy or stupid. They may be frustrated with their uncoordinated efforts so that emotional problems and low self-esteem are not an uncommon result. They may also be socially immature (just under 50% of Henderson and Hall's group were), though this may be as a result of their clumsiness, which has meant a degree of social isolation.

Remediation   There has been much written on the subject of training in the perceptual-motor area, which has been already covered. The main theoretical contribution has come from the work of Kephart who attempted to develop the perceptual-motor match by progressively moving from the development of large motor skills to fine ones. Many of Kephart's ideas have been incorporated into the remedial programs given below. Gordon and McKinlay (1980), following the work of Arnheim and Sinclair (1975), surveyed the gross motor skills to be taught under nine categories, which were:-

1. Tension release - systematic muscle tension and release exercises, breathing exercises, yoga and breadmaking.

2. Locomotion - rocking, crawling, creeping, walking, jumping, skipping.

3. Balance - standing on one or two feet, balance beam exercises, heel-toe walking.

4. Body awareness - moving and pointing to various parts of the body both on self and other person. Unilateral and cross-lateral movements.

5. Rhythm exercises - rebound and airborne activities, skipping, trampoline work and dance.

6. Ball management - rolling, throwing, catching and bouncing with balls and other objects.

7. Management of daily activities - sorting tasks, stringing beads, placing and pasting, pegboard and blackboard activities.

8. Play skills - roller skating, bicycle riding, swimming, skipping etc.

9. Motor fitness - standard P.E. exercises for strength, agility, speed and power.

Gordon and Grimley (1974) also covered activities for fine motor skill development and tactile discrimination:

1. Modelling with clay, 'play-doh', plasticine etcetera.

2. Painting, including finger painting.

3. Sand modelling and drawing.

4. Discrimination by the shape and feel of objects.

5. Bead threading and lacing cards.

6. Constructive toys and games.

7. Dot-to-dot and writing exercises.

8. Pegboard exercises.

9. Activities with sandpaper and felt letters and shapes.

10. Water play.

Although all these activities may be useful, they are no more than those readily available in the infant and junior school. Presumably, if such activities are to be used for remediation, the activities should be graded in order of difficulty and carried through with much repetition and in small steps, in much the same manner as the programme devised by Frostig et al (1973).

HYPERACTIVITY OR DIFFICULTY WITH ATTENTION AND ACTIVITY LEVEL

As already indicated, there is considerable disagreement about the use of the term 'hyperactive'. Not only are the estimates of numbers of hyperactive children variable, but some of the methods of treatment are extreme and possibly dangerous.

The term 'hyperactive' derived from the work of Strauss and Lehtinen (1947) who first described the brain-injured child as one who was impulsive and easily distracted. Today the term 'hyperactivity' or 'hyperkinesis' has subsumed the term 'brain-injured child', but still carries with it the implication of brain damage. Whaley and Malott (1971) describes a hyperactive child thus:

> Earl's hyperactivity took the form of talking, pushing, hitting, pinching, looking about the classroom and out the window, leaving his desk, tapping, squirming, and fiddling with objects. In addition he was aggressive, pinched other children, and threw himself into groups of children, disrupting their work or play. One extreme form of disruptive behavior which he occasionally engaged in was shoving of his desk around the classroom, pushing aside all the children and desks in his way. Because Earl was an aggressive nine-year-old in a classroom of seven-year-olds, the other children consciously avoided him.

Ross and Ross (1976) and Farnham-Diggory (1978) following the work of Stewart, Pitts, Craig and Pierfu (1966) give the following as criteria for the definition of hyperactivity. The child must be overactive, that is, he must demonstrate an abnormal amount of energy and restlessness. He or she must also show symptoms of distractability, including never finishing work or projects. In addition, six out of a total of 24 other symptoms should be demonstrated.

These criteria are probably due to be replaced by the operational and temporary criteria given by DSM III (in the USA). According to Shaywitz and Shaywitz (1984), DSM III delineates two possible syndromes which are attention deficit disorder (ADD) and attention deficit disorder with hyperactivity (ADD-H). For a diagnosis of ADD the child must demonstrate the following symptoms of inattention and impulsivity.

101

<u>Inattention</u> Four of the following must be demonstrated:

1. Needs calm quiet atmosphere to work or is unable to work.

2. Frequently asks for things to be repeated.

3. Easily distracted.

4. Confuses details.

5. Does not finish what he starts.

6. Hears but does not seem to listen.

7. Difficulty concentrating unless in a one-to-one situation.

<u>Impulsivity</u> Three of the following must be demonstrated:

1. Calls out in class or makes noise in class.

2. Is extremely excitable.

3. Has trouble waiting his turn.

4. Talks excessively.

5. Disrupts other children.

For the additional diagnosis of hyperactivity the following symptoms are necessary:

<u>Hyperactivity</u> Three of the following must be demonstrated:

1. Climbs onto cabinets and furniture.

2. Is always on the go, would run rather than walk.

3. Fidgets or squirms.

4. Does things in a loud and noisy way.

5. Must be doing something or fidgets.

    Other criteria include the fact that it has an onset below the age of seven years and has had a duration of at least six months. There may also be accompanying side effects, for example insomnia or sleep disturbance, decrease in appetite and weight loss.

The main symptom for hyperactivity can be subsumed under the label overactivity. Yet it is this particular label that has presented the most difficulty. As Ross (1977) comments:

> What is meant by the term 'hyperactive'? No more than that someone has decided that the child so labeled moves about more than the observer deems normal. Since there is no standard by which one might judge the normal activity level of a child of a given age, the designation of hyperactive is based on many subjective factors. It has a lot to do with the expectations and tolerance level of the adults who judge a child's behaviour. Like other behaviours that are classed together by a descriptive label, overly active behaviour not only comes in many degrees of magnitude but is also likely to have several different causes. Since activity level is a normal human characteristic it, like other characteristics, will vary from one individual to the next. Some people are short, some tall, many of medium size. One should not be surprised to find some children are mildly lethargic, some quite active, and many somewhere in between. Just as we would not say that a person whose size is near the upper end of the normal range of weight is therefore sick, so we should not attach a label which sounds like an illness to a child whose activity level is near the upper end of the normal range of body movement.

Another problem is that the hyperactive child is often first brought to attention because of poor behaviour. Some researchers, for example Shaffer, McNamara and Pincus (1974); say the problem is often confused with conduct disorder. But others, for example Whalen and Henker (1980), see bad behaviour, including aggression, as a likely secondary problem. In a study of five- to seven-year-old boys, Shaffer et al (1974) found that boys who had been referred to a psychiatric clinic for conduct disorder showed higher levels of activity (as measured by an actometer) than boys without conduct disorder. The real problem is that hyperactivity is seen as a problem caused by minimal brain damage. Most of the children with conduct disorder in the cases studied had no evidence of neurological involvement and their bad behaviour was likely to be caused by social and environmental circumstances. From such research it seems likely that the diagnosis of hyperactivity in a child does not imply that the child has minimal brain damage. It is likely that there is considerable overlap between hyperactivity and conduct disorder.

This brings us to the area of major disagreement in causation of hyperactivity. On the one hand there are those who view it as one end of the continuum of normal behaviour (Shrag and Divoky, 1981), on the other there are those who consider it to have a neurological basis. This latter idea stems from the work of Strauss and Lehtinen (1947) who studied the brain damaged child and concluded this was a child who is impulsive and distractable. More recent theorists suggest that there is an abnormality in neurotransmitter functions. More specifically, there is thought to be a deficit in the metabolism of monoamines, namely in seratonin and noradrenaline. One suggestion is that there is a lack of inhibition of neurological transmission due to a deficiency in the production of this substance at brain level. Some findings point to this deficiency in that there is an increase in certain metabolites in the blood of hyperactive children (Raskin, 1984). Note that in another study, Shaywitz, Grossman and Shaywitz (1984), there was a failure to replicate these findings. However, the inhibition of neurological transmission hypothesis is attractive in that it would explain some of the behaviour of hyperactive children. The biochemical abnormality would have effects which are as follows. Firstly, that there is a resulting impairment in the neural mechanism of the brain so the hyperactive child has a diminished experience of pleasure and pain. The second effect would be on the activation system of the brain which is exacerbated and poorly modulated so that activity is inappropriate. The theory is also attractive in that it explains why certain drugs are effective in the treatment of hyperactive children, which is covered in the next section.

Such problems of the definition and causation of hyperactivity are partly related to difficulties in the measurement of hyperactivity. Just what a normal level of activity is is quite difficult to judge. However, there are various techniques developing, such as heartbeat monitors, underfloor pressure points and actometers (measuring muscle activity) which might make such measurement easier (see Holt, 1975). Many of these techniques are not available to the classroom teacher who must rely perhaps on the list of symptoms given here, referring any questionable cases to the educational psychologist.

The learning capacity of the hyperactive child is profoundly affected by the cumulative affects of short attention span. There will be an increase in the gap between intelligence and achievement in mathematics, reading and spelling so that the child becomes more and more retarded. The child increasingly expects to fail which effects his or her level of confidence, self-esteem and general personality. Ross and Ross (1976) state:

Hyperactivity profoundly effects the personal and academic life of the individual child. Long term psychological, academic and remedial assistance would be required if these effects were to be avoided.

Battle and Lacey (1972) note that the psychological effects on the personality of hyperactivity is different at different age levels. Below the age of three years the child is merely non-compliant. From three to six years of age the child is very physical and avoids academic activity. Later on, in the junior school, the child begins to note that he is failing and is more compliant to adults. But at this age the child is often very aggressive to his peers. In his early teens the child is beginning to note his failure more and worry about this. He becomes increasingly anxious about this lack of achievement and his self-esteem is lowered.

Treatment   Ways of treating hyperactivity are quite varied. Though the most effective and popular treatment is by the use of stimulant drugs, this is decreasing in popularity and other behavioural treatments are gaining place.
The main drug used for the control of hyperactivity is Ritalan (i.e. amphetamine). This is a stimulant drug, but it has a complex effect on the balance between nervous excitation and inhibition, which is adequately explained by Farnham-Diggory (1978). There are those (Ross and Ross, 1976) who are quite sceptical of its use and possible overuse. They report that 2% of elementary school children in the USA were receiving such medication in 1970-71. It is also known that the drug has quite severe side effects such as anorexia, insomnia, growth suppression and increase in heart rate. In addition to these possibly dangerous side effects the drug does not seem to be as effective as once thought. It does improve attention and learning in the short term, but it has no long term effect on achievement. It decreases interpersonal friction and hostility in the short term, but does not have a consistent effect on the number of aggressive or antisocial acts (Whalen and Henker, 1980).

Hence, drug control is not a simple effective treatment for hyperactivity and probably gives rise to as many problems as it cures.

Forms of behaviour therapy have also been quite popular in treating hyperactivity. Young children especially have responded well to the 'ignore and praise' regime (Brown and Elliot, 1965) where the child's positive useful acts are praised and hostile and aggressive acts are ignored. Young children who have these problems would not be described as hyperactive, but simply as children who 'act out' or have behaviour problems. Sometimes a type of punishment is used, where the child is withdrawn from social contact (Herbert, 1981) and this is most effective in the treatment of this problem. For older children a more structured approach is required, for example in the engineered classroom developed by Hewett (1967, 1969).

Cognitive-behavioural strategies are now gaining ground, as a form of treatment. The main principle behind such therapy is that the child should be encouraged to take control of his or her own behaviour. Utilising the three stages of the initiation and inhibition of voluntary behaviour proposed by Luria (1966), Ross and Ross (1976) have assisted hyperactive children in taking up control of their own treatment. The idea is to find out which of Luria's stages the child is at and then to attempt to teach him or her the next stage. These three stages are:

1. The child's behaviour is controlled and directed by the speech of others.

2. The child begins to use overt speech to regulate behaviour effectively.

3. Covert or inner speech takes over.

Hyperactive children are usually taught, firstly, to 'talk over' their actions and later, to talk to themselves about it. For such self direction the child has to 'Stop, look, listen and think'. A similar type of effective behaviour management is proposed by Meichenbaum (1975).

A fairly recent and controversial area in the treatment of hyperactivity is alteration of diet. The idea that the hyperactive child is allergic to certain kinds of foodstuffs has gained in popularity. Feingold (1975) was one of the first to point out that children could be reacting adversely to food colourants and preservatives, wheat and even cow's milk. Children were put on exclusion diets based on the following principles:

a) Exclusion of synthetic colours and flavours.

b) Exclusion of two vegetables and 21 fruits.

c) Exclusion of certain non-foods, e.g. toothpaste and mouthwashes.

Feingold claimed that 50% of hyperactive children improved on such a diet.

Some researchers (Golden, 1984) have been quite critical of the claim that food additives produce hyperactivity. Certain research studies have shown no demonstrable effect of food additives. One group of researchers in this area are Harley, Ray and Tomasi (1978). They carried out a double blind experiment in that 50% of hyperactive children were put on an exclusion diet and 50% were put on another kind of diet. Researchers assessing the hyperactivity did not know which children were receiving which diets. Such studies failed to demonstrate that these substances had any effect.

More recently, however, research has demonstrated that certain substances can provoke hyperactivity. In a double blind, crossover placebo controlled trial, foods which were thought to produce symptoms were gradually introduced to 28 hyperactive children (Egger, Carter, Graham, Gumley and Soothill, 1985). Symptoms were rated independently by parents and psychologists and were found to be exacerbated when the children were eating the active materials rather than placebo foods. The active substance in these cases were mostly colourants and preservatives (particularly tartrazine), cow's milk, chocolate, grapes, wheat, oranges and cow's cheese. All of these substances were reacted to adversely by 40% or more of the children. The 28 children were a subgroup of a total sample of 76 hyperactive children and were selected because they appeared to have some adverse reaction to these substances in a pilot study. This would seem to imply that slightly over a third of hyperactive children might be so affected. Also the diet is not as simple as this account would suggest, because of the use of colourants and preservatives in modern day foods. It is costly, unpalatable and inconvenient.

Although this last study would seem to indicate that diet has some effect on hyperactivity, there are other studies where no effect is found. Also, diet does not appear to have any effect on some children's hyperactivity. So we must keep an open mind on the subject which has not as yet given conclusive results. Parents may be misguided into thinking diet is responsible for the behaviour of their child when in fact it is not, and embark on costly and ineffective treatment by unqualified people.

SUMMARY

This is a widely divergent chapter in that learning difficulties in the visual-motor are covered alongside hyperactivity, which might be considered as a kind of 'motor' problem. Two of the learning difficulties covered (clumsiness and hyperactivity) are ones which are beginning to be attended to. But they are also areas where there is considerable dearth of knowledge regarding the incidence, identification, causation and remediation of the learning difficulty. This is particularly true in the area of hyperactivity. We can but hope that the next few years will bring some fruitful research in these areas which might result in a consolidation of opinion.

6. DIFFICULTIES IN MATHEMATICS

Backwardness in the area of arithmetic and mathematics has long given cause for concern. Schonell (1937) wrote about 'the extreme importance of sound foundations in arithmetic' and the need for early diagnosis of arithmetic problems in order to prevent 'far-reaching emotional handicaps'. He recognised the interplay of cognitive and emotional factors in the area of mathematics which has since been emphasised in the work of Skemp (1971) and Cockroft (1982).

This concern has been reflected in a proliferation of research reports and projects. In the sixties we had an emphasis on developing understanding in mathematics together with a change in educational methods in the primary school with the Plowden Report (1967) and the Nuffield Mathematics Project (1966-69). Throughout the seventies and continuing to the present day we have various assessments of mathematics attainment and teaching by the Assessment of Performance Unit (Foxman, Gresswell, Ward, Badger, Tusan and Bloomfield, 1978; Foxman, Ruddoch, Badger and Martini, 1980) and the National Foundation for Educational Research and Schools Council (Choat, 1980; Denvir, Stolz and Brown, 1982; Ward, 1979) culminating in the Cockroft Report of 1982. And yet, despite all this effort, we have little information on the incidence of backwardness in mathematics. We can say that there are fewer mathematics 'O' levels and CSE's than there are in other subjects (Cockroft, 1982; Pidgeon, 1967). One third of all school children leave school with no 'O' level or CSE in mathematics. Boys are higher attainers than girls at the end of schooling at least as far as mathematics is concerned (Shuard and Quadling, 1980) but there is little information on attainment throughout the child's school career.

The meagre information on the incidence of difficulties in mathematics is as follows. The Isle of Wight survey of Rutter, Tizard and Whitmore (1970) found that children who were poor at reading were also poor at arithmetic. Pringle, Butler and Davie (1966), in a survey of 11,000 seven-year-olds, found 3.6% of these children showed little or no mathematical understanding. The DES report (1978) on mathematical attainment in 11-year-olds found that 9.6% obtained scores of 14 or less on a test where the average score was 28. The study also indicated that 10 to 15% of 11-year-olds had difficulty with counting and adding accurately when using groups of tens and units.

The lack of information on the incidence of backwardness in mathematics may be due to the changing view of the nature of mathematics and hence the changing nature of standardised tests. Today's mathematics tests are very different from the 1950 tests of the Schonell's which covered the four basic processes. The second reason is that there seems to be enormous variability in mathematics achievement. Cockroft (1982) gives the example of the problem of writing the number which is one greater than 6399. Most 11-year-olds can do this but there are some 14-year-olds who cannot and some 7-year-olds who can. As the incidence problem is connected to the problem of classifying mathematical difficulties, let us examine this latter difficulty in detail.

THE CLASSIFICATION OF LEARNING DIFFICULTIES IN MATHEMATICS

The Nature of Learning Difficulties in Mathematics

The classification of learning difficulties in mathematics is by no means clear-cut as there are many different views on the nature of mathematical difficulties. On the one hand we have many educationalists who see mathematics as a difficult area where children fail for a variety of reasons, including anxiety, lack of experience, poor teaching and cultural deprivation (Cockroft, 1982; Denvir, Stolz and Brown, 1982). On the other hand we have those research psychologists who classify the learning disabilities of children in accordance with brain-damaged adults calling the children acalculic or dyscalculic (Farnham-Diggory, 1978). Because of the lack of consensus and the disparate categories used, any classification of learning difficulties in mathematics is in the nature of a working hypothesis, though one based on the relevant research literature. It is not necessary to think of the proposed categories as discrete, or of a particular child belonging to one category and not another. Rather, in the spirit of the Warnock Report (1978) one can think of learning difficulties in mathematics as learning difficulties in specific skills or abilities. This view is also the one proposed by Tansley and Pankhurst (1981). Any one child may have more than one specific learning difficulty.

One of the problems encountered in attempting to classify learning difficulties in mathematics is that many mathematical computations require for their solution the operation of a number of different skills or abilities. Cohn (1961) points out that long multiplication calls for:

1) Recognition of symbol
2) Long term memory (for tables)
3) Working memory (carrying)
4) Ability to order results
5) A final addition with carrying

A child may get the answer wrong through being unable to perform any one of these operations or several of them. Different mathematical skills and abilities are involved, for example reading and writing numbers and symbols, computational ability involving memory with spatial ability. Learning disabilities occur in all of these areas and will be covered by the proposed classification.

In addition persons may solve the same problem using different methods. To use an example of Krutetskii (1976), when considering the problem 'How much does a brick weigh if it weighs 1kg and half a brick?', one child may solve the problem algebraically and write:

$$x = 1+1/2x$$
$$x-1/2x = 1$$
$$1/2x = 1$$
$$x = 2$$

A second child solves the problem using diagrams:

One brick weighs 2kg.

A third child may use verbal reasoning and state 'The difference between a brick and a half a brick is half a brick, which must weigh 1kg. Therefore a brick weighs 2kg.' Yet a fourth child may see the solution intuitively and present the correct answer without quite knowing why. These children may be said to be using different mathematical styles, these are algebraic, spatial, verbal and intuitive respectively. Persons who exhibit a consistent preference for a certain style of

111

solution would be said to be a certain mathematical type. Krutetskii has identified four such types, analytic (abstract or algebraic), geometric (visual or spatial), harmonic-abstract and harmonic-visual, the last two being less extreme versions of the analytic and geometric types.

This work on mathematical types is reinforced by research on the structure of mathematical ability. From the work of Thurstone (1938) and others as reviewed by Krutetskii (1976), there is evidence for the following specific abilities, all of which may be involved in the subject called mathematics.

General ability (G)   - Underlies most mathematical abilities except computation.

Numerical ability (N)   - Strongly related to computation.

Spatial ability (S)   - An important factor in geometry.

Verbal ability (V)   - An important factor in mathematical problem solving and algebra.

Reasoning (R) and
Memory (M)   - Both are found to be related to mathematics in general.

There is evidence that mathematical reasoning (R) and verbal/abstract abilities (V) appear later in development than general, numerical and spatial abilities (Osborn, 1983). Much of the research on the development of mathematical abilities is of an entirely different nature. For example, Piaget's (1953) work on the development of the number concept, Skemp's (1971) work on mathematical understanding and Krutetskii's (1976) ideas on mathematical development. These theorists look at the nature of mathematics as a process rather than a product, and stress the importance of understanding in mathematics. This is covered in a later section.

Specific and General Mathematics Disability

Specific mathematical disability, like specific reading disability, can be seen as a problem which occurs in children of otherwise average ability. The degree of backwardness in mathematics should be between one-and-a-half and two years in a child of at least average intelligence and good background. Mathematical disability also can arise as just one disability amongst many in a child who is generally backward because of lower intelligence, poor educational background or both.

Specific mathematical disability (acalculia or dyscalculia) is recognised by many clinicians, including Luria (1966), Johnson and Myklebust (1967) and Critchley (1970), but in the field of education many researchers (e.g. Denvir et al, 1982; Pidgeon, 1967; Skemp, 1971) make no reference to it. Those who do make reference to specific mathematical disability seem to attribute any retardation to factors other than cognitive ones. For example, Cockcroft (1982) refers to the fact that 'low attainment can occur in children whose general ability is not low', but the reasons given for such retardation were 'inappropriate teaching, lack of confidence, lack of opportunity, frequent or prolonged illness and poor reading skills'. These factors may all be important, but there may also be underlying learning disabilities of a cognitive nature which need to be remedied. The Schools Council Working Paper (Denvir et al, 1982) also makes no reference to specific mathematical disability, a fact aptly brought to our attention by Joffe (1983), who refers to this as 'a disappointing feature' of the report. It is also a reflection of the lack of research on the subject that Tansley and Pankhurst (1981), in a book on Specific Learning Difficulties, can find only enough research to cover two pages in the area of disability in arithmetic. Nor is this omission confined to Great Britain. Weinstein (1980) also refers to the fact that many researchers in the USA take for granted the factors of 'inadequate instruction, poor motivation or general mental retardation' when referring to low attainment in mathematics, but fail to look for cognitive factors. Again in the USA there is a dearth of research on the subject.

But do these children with specific mathematical disability actually exist? Is it possible that children who are retarded in mathematics have a general backwardness in all subjects? Certainly Tansley and Pankhurst (1981) claim that there is insufficient evidence whether 'poor arithmetic performance is associated with specific learning disabilities'. As far as incidence of specific mathematical disabilities is concerned again (like general mathematical disability) we have few figures. The largest survey of specific mathematical disability to date has been carried out by Kosc (1974) in Czechoslovakia and he gives an incidence of 6% in children of 11 years of age. Badian (1983), in a survey of the literature on the subject, also gives a figure of 6% based largely on research by Madden, Gardner, Rudman, Karlsen and Merwin (1973). From this it would appear that, whereas 6.4% of school children have a disability in mathematics, only 3.7% of children have a disability in mathematics alone, the remaining 2.7% having a disability in both mathematics and reading. However, neither of these studies give precise information about the level of backwardness and the test used is often not standardised. So these incidence figures must be taken as rough estimates only.

As mentioned before, children of normal intelligence who have a specific reading disability may also have a disability in mathematics. Tansley and Pankhurst (1981) refer to the fact that some poor readers are also below average in mathematics but 'the precise nature of the association is not clear'. It is not clear, for example, whether the children have a problem reading the numbers or not. Joffe (1980) found that 61% of dyslexic children (children with specific reading disability) were not achieving in arithmetic at a level commensurate with their chronological age, despite average or above average intelligence. In a study of dyslexic children aged 7 to 18 years, Miles (1983) found that many of them were inaccurate on items such as subtraction, knowledge of tables and reciting months of the year. For example, of the 80 children in the 9- to 12-year-old age group 58% scored significantly more errors in substraction, 96% scored significantly more errors in knowledge of tables and 60% scored significantly more errors in reciting the months of the year, than average readers. The association between mathematics and reading disability is probably dependent on the type of mathematics being undertaken, whether verbal problem solving or a geometric puzzle to give two extremes.

It is likely that there is not just one type of specific reading disability (Boder, 1973; Johnson and Myklebust, 1967). Similarly, it seems likely that specific mathematical disability is not a unitary deficit. Certainly Rourke (1978) and Badian (1983) refer to many types of acalculia (specific disability in mathematics). Myklebust (1980), when writing about learning disabilities in general, considers them to be a heterogeneous group. Badian (1983) suggests that we need more precise differentiation among subgroups of children if we are to progress in our understanding and remediation of learning disabilities in mathematics.

A classification of difficulties in mathematics is summarised below. This is largely based on suggestions of Badian (1983) at least as far as specific difficulties are concerned. Higher order difficulties in mathematics have been added.

Figure 6.1: Proposed Classification of Difficulties in Mathematics

---

Specific difficulties in mathematics
  (a) Difficulty with reading and writing numbers
  (b) Difficulty with calculations
  (c) Spatial difficulties

Higher order difficulties in mathematics
  (a) Difficulty in understanding mathematics
  (b) Difficulty with the language of mathematics

Specific Difficulties in Mathematics

Specific difficulties in mathematics are those which clinicians and educationalists have noticed as occurring in children as isolated phenomena. That is, a child may exhibit a particular difficulty and have no other difficulty in the area of mathematics or any other subject. However, in many cases such learning difficulties are not seen in isolation. A child may have difficulty with reading and writing numbers and calculation, for example. As I have already mentioned, the classificatory basis is not well established at the present time.

Difficulty with Reading and Writing Numbers

This is referred to by some clinicians as number alexia and may show itself in one of two ways. Either, the child has difficulty with numbers (e.g. writing 3 as $\mathcal{E}$), or the child has a problem with signs and symbols (e.g. reading 3 + 5 as 3 x 5). The problem is quite commonly seen in children who have an additional reading difficulty (Critchley, 1970; Joffe, 1980; Johnson and Myklebust, 1967; Miles, 1983; Spellacy and Peters, 1978). However, many dyslexics have fewer difficulties with arithmetic than with reading. This is due to the fact that each number has only one numerical symbol (e.g. '8') whereas words contain a sequence of letters (e.g. 'eight'). In reading words there may be great difficulty in remembering the sequence of sounds and their associated symbols, whereas in arithmetic each number word has but one symbol, although, of course, there may be problems with number sequences such as 432. So, the number difficulty is not often seen beyond the age of seven or eight and may account for the lack of cases reported by some researchers (Badian, 1983).

Johnson and Myklebust (1967) note that the difficulty with reading and writing numbers mostly affects the numbers 2, 3, 5, 6 and 9. This is probably because 2 and 5 are confusable with S, 6 and 9 are confusable with each other and 3 confuses with E. Note that mirror images of symbols are a source of confusion here. The disturbance may also effect calculations, because a child cannot remember the appearance of numbers (e.g. writing 2 for 5). One 9-year-old could do written work only with a wall clock available so that he could read the numbers. In older children written errors occur with more difficult notation. Joffe (1980) found that children wrote 'one pound and five-and-a-half pence' in several different erroneous forms.

Researchers into mathematical difficulties do not always differentiate number writing problems from computational disability (Rourke and Finlayson, 1978; Rourke and Strang, 1978; Spellacy and Peters, 1978). One might speculate that the disability involves a deficiency in the verbal factor, though it might also be a visual problem. It is interesting to note that in adults the difficulty is associated with left (dominant) hemisphere brain damage, as are calculation difficulties (Benson and Weir, 1972; Boller and Graffman, 1983; Hecaen, 1962). It seems likely then that a problem with reading and writing numbers is not usually an isolated difficulty.

Remediation Remedial procedures are discussed by Johnson and Myklebust (1967) at some length. One method is to let the child compensate for his problem by supplying a chart showing the numbers whilst the child is performing calculations. The introduction of multiple-choice questions, where the child has only to encircle the correct answer can be given to alleviate the tedium of continuous copying. Then practise in reading and writing numbers can be carried out at a different time. Exercises, similar to those given to children with problems in reading and writing letters (see earlier chapter) can also be given. Orientation, for example, can be helped by an exercise in which the child has to pick the odd one out in a series, as shown below:

```
3   3   Ɛ   3
6   6   6   ∂
ح   2   2   2
5   ح   5   5
```

The child can trace felt numbers, use clay and sand trays and trace number forms at the same time as saying the number. Whole sequences of number activities involving feedback from the various senses (vision, hearing, muscle sense and touch) can be designed in a manner reminiscent of the VAKT technique used in remedial reading (Gillingham and Stillman, 1956). The child can also be taught number rhymes to say whilst writing a number. For example, when writing the number 5 he or she might say: 'Here's a man ('), with a fat tummy (5). Now put his hat on (5)'.

Difficulties with Calculations

Calculation difficulties are quite common in children and may occur in any child because of a temporary memory lapse. On the other hand, there are children who seem unable to learn how to perform certain calculations, making the same mistakes repeatedly. Difficulty with calculation is also known as anarithmetica (Badian, 1983).

As with the difficulty in reading and writing numbers the problem often occurs in children with an additional reading difficulty (Joffe, 1980; Rourke and Finlayson, 1978; Spellacy and Peters, 1978), though it can occur in isolation. From studies of adults with dyscalculia, the left (dominant) hemisphere (in particular the parietal region) would seem to be involved in calculation. From Thurstone's (1938) work there would seem to be a separate factor (N) which is strongly related to calculation and arithmetic.

Ward's (1979) survey showed that many 10-year-olds have problems with calculation. Simple addition sums as, for example, 238 + 375 are correctly answered by the majority of children (87%). Subtraction is slightly more difficult with the sum 439 - 284 being correctly computed by 70% of children. The major source of error (in 11% of children) is due to a mistake in carrying over a digit from the tens column giving an answer of 255 instead of 155. Multiplication proved even more difficult, only 55% of children getting the correct answer for the sum 283 x 7. Most of the mistakes were in the lack of knowledge of tables and mistakes with carrying. Division sums were also very difficult. Only 43% of the children had the sum 255 ÷ 6 correct. Again mistakes were due to lack of knowledge of tables and in carrying. Calculations involving written problems, fractions or decimals were even more difficult, but most difficult of all were sums involving change of format. For example, the problem:

Write the missing number in the division sum

$$\div\ 4\ =\ 14$$

was correctly answered by only 33% of 10-year-olds. Many children gave the answer as three-and-a-half because they had divided 14 by 4. In a problem of this type, children tried to work out the answer with the elements provided regardless of the sense of the problem.

In the study of four dyscalculia children aged between 14 and 16 and a half years, Slade and Russell (1971) also found multiplication to be a more difficult operation than addition or subtraction. In these cases the relative deficiency in multiplication stemmed from a faulty grasp of multiplication tables. In general, long mathematical problems cause difficulty for children with a calculation problem as they require the child to retain a number of operations and to apply them in correct sequence as in the example of long multiplication referred to earlier. Children are usually incorrect with a calculation for one of the two reasons already mentioned, either they confuse or misapply arithmetical operations or they have a memory problem and make mistakes when calculating. These two problems will be dealt with in turn.

Confusion and Misapplication of Operations Denvir et al (1982) provide an example of a 12-year-old girl who confused operations. The girl, who was a pupil in a comprehensive school, had completed correctly 30 sums of the type:

$$\begin{array}{r} 25 \\ \times\ 3 \\ \hline 75 \end{array}$$

The next row of her sum book began:

$$\begin{array}{r} 53 \\ \times\ 7 \\ \hline 491 \end{array}$$

Here the girl has multiplied 3 x 7 and obtained the result 21. She has then added the 2 to 5 to obtain 7 and multiplied this by 7 to obtain 49. All the sums on this row were incorrect because of this mistake in carrying over the tens. Either, she was confusing a multiplication operation with an addition operation, or she may have had two operations in the incorrect sequence of addition followed by multiplication (5 + 2 = 7, 7 + 7 = 49) instead of multiplication followed by addition (5 x 7 = 35, 35 + 2 = 37).

A second example is given by Joffe (1980) in which

118

a child begins by selecting the correct operation and then changes to another one half way through the calculation.

```
  236
x   5   Multiplication changed to addition?
  380
```

```
  357   Initial addition changed to
-  89   subtraction and number
  476   carried incorrectly.
```

Carrying and re-grouping errors also occur in this context, especially when there is confusion over the number to be carried. Two examples are given by Joffe:

```
   57
x   8   The child carries 10 instead of 50
  416
```

```
   42   The child has incorrectly multiplied
x   9   9 x 2 and obtained 18, but has
  441   carried the wrong number (8 instead of 1)
```

In this context it is pertinent to refer to Resnick and Ford's (1981) account of children's algorithms. According to them any computation is performed by recall of certain number facts and knowledge of a fixed sequence of operations called algorithms. For example, given the sum:

$$348$$
$$+ 59$$

This is performed by the following algorithm:

1. Add (8 + 9)
2. Notate (7)
3. Carry (1)
4. Add (1 + 4 + 5)
5. Notate (0)
6. Carry (1)
7. Add (1 + 3)
8. Notate (4)

The number facts are:

1. 8 + 9 = 17
2. 1 + 4 + 5 = 10
3. 3 + 1 = 4

The more complex a computation (as in long multiplication or division) the more complex the algorithm (and often the more difficult the number facts that one has to recall). Some children quite simply make computational errors because they have incorrectly stated these algorithms or they are confusing algorithms. For example, they may confuse the algorithm of addition for that of subtraction. These incorrect algorithms are sometimes referred to as mathematical bugs (Brown and Burton, 1978), an example of one being given by the series of computations below:

7	9	17	87	365	679	923	27,493
+ 8	+ 5	+ 8	+ 93	+ 514	+ 794	+ 481	+ 1,509
15	14	25	11	819	111	114	28,991

The bug in the procedure is that, whenever the number is to be carried to the next column, the child writes down the tens digit (which should be carried) and simply ignores the units digit. This is due to an incorrect algorithm, or a mistake in the execution of the algorithm. No operations have been confused here. An incorrect algorithm which is due to confused operations is given by the failing attempts at a sum performed by Badian (1983). This 11-year-old boy, who was of average intelligence, made several attempts at the same sum, being correct at the fourth attempt.

1.
$$\begin{array}{r} 309 \\ + 106 \\ \hline 903 \\ 309 \\ \underline{319} \\ 3 \end{array}$$
Confusion of addition and long multiplication
Subtraction instead of addition (9 - 6 = 3)
Addition of zero

2.
$$\begin{array}{r} 309 \\ + 106 \\ \hline 963 \end{array}$$
Subtraction (9 - 6)
Addition (0 + 6, 3 + 6)

3.
$$\begin{array}{r} 309 \\ + 106 \\ \hline 203 \end{array}$$
Subtraction

4.
$$\begin{array}{r} 309 \\ + 106 \\ \hline 415 \end{array}$$
Correct

Many children have incorrect algorithms or mathematical bugs which are completely overlooked.

Unfortunately they may repeatedly get sums wrong by performing the same incorrect algorithms, and these incorrect algorithms become more and more firmly established. The child's mathematical bug can be found by careful observation and analysis of incorrect sums over a period of time, just as in the examples given here.

Remediation   When the child has difficulties with calculations which are due to confusion of operations (incorrect algorithms), the child needs to be taught the correct algorithms by a remedial procedure which should include many opportunities for practise of the correct procedure. In this context Brown and Burton (1978) have developed a computer programme 'Buggy', which helps to identify and remediate such bugs in children's individual computations. The rationale is to have a mental map of the sequence of operations involved in particular computations and to show where the child is likely to go wrong.
    Such an information processing model of computation has been developed by Gagné (1970) and Resnick and Ford (1981). Gagné (1970) and Gagné and Briggs (1974) refer to learning hierarchies, the one for subtraction being given here (Figure 6.2). Each of the subskills in the hierarchy should be mastered in turn. If they are not then this can lead to a child developing incorrect algorithms. By analysis of a task (such as subtraction) into a correct learning hierarchy and by observation of the child's errors, it is possible to pinpoint the stage in the hierarchy that the child has reached. Teaching can then begin at this or the next stage. There is insufficient space here to do justice to the works of Gagné, and Resnick and Ford, but the reader is referred to their work and to the case given at the end of the section on understanding mathematics.

Retention or Memory Problem   Two types of error are common, firstly forgetting multiplication tables, and secondly forgetting to carry or pay back in a computation. This second type can be thought of as forgetting of part of the algorithm as mentioned earlier. Badian (1983) refers to attentional-sequential dyscalculia in which children with this sort of problem are discussed, but there seems to be little evidence that this is a discrete type.
    Forgetting of multiplication tables is quite common in children with reading difficulties. According to Miles (1970) many such children claimed to 'know their

Figure 6.2: A learning hierarchy for subtracting whole numbers (Gagné and Briggs, 1974)

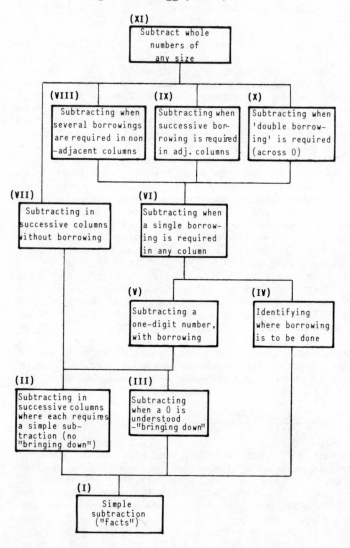

tables', but produced answers such as 7 x 8 = 64, 5 x 7 = 25. One child produced the same answer to two questions, that is, 7 x 8 = 56 and 6 x 8 = 56 and saw 'nothing wrong in it'. Miles (1983) notes the following types of error made by dyslexic children who, despite 'long and hard efforts', still made mistakes when reciting tables:

i) Loss of place (e.g. 'Was it six sevens I was up to?')

ii) Consistent errors in which a correct deduction is made from a faulty premise (e.g. 'two eights are fifteen, three eights are twenty-three')

iii) A variety of slips such as changing from one table to another (e.g. 'six eights are forty-eight, nine sevens are sixty-three')

iv) The adoption of compensatory strategies such as taking up what was said earlier in order to get back on course (e.g. 'Once two is two; two twos are four; three ---- two twos are four; three twos are six'), and saying the table without the preamble (e.g. 'two, four, six, eight, etc.')

Carrying errors are seen in the following sums:

$$\begin{array}{r} 29 \\ + \underline{56} \\ \underline{75} \end{array}$$ Forgetting to add the carried number

$$\begin{array}{r} 31 \\ - \underline{9} \\ \underline{32} \end{array}$$ Forgetting to pay back the borrowed number

Badian (1983) gives this example of a 13-year-old boy who forgets decimal points when carrying:

$$\begin{array}{r} 3.95 \\ \times \underline{3} \\ \underline{1275} \end{array}$$

Memory is important for a number of other mathematical operations. As the mathematical problem gets more difficult, the memory factor is more important as the child has to retain more and more information 'in his head'. Badian notes that some children are quite capable of performing single arithmetic operations, for example 7 x 8 = 56, but may seem to be unable to carry out this operation when it is involved in a more complex sum (say long multiplication), because of the additional memory load.

One test devised by Luria (1966) which emphasises

the memory factor is that of successively subtracting 7 from 100. Here it is necessary to keep in mind the result of the operation which becomes the starting point of the next operation. This test was used by Kosc (1974) in his study of 66 dyscalculic children, and he found that the poorest results were obtained by children who had additional verbal difficulties, rather than those who had spatial difficulties.

Resnick and Ford (1981) stress the role of memory in computation when discussing the correct execution of algorithms (mathematical procedures). Working memory, as the name suggests, carries out all the computational activity retrieving, as it does, so many necessary number facts (e.g. 7 x 8 = 56) from long term memory. During long calculations much of working memory will tend to be occupied in keeping place in a long procedure and holding the numbers needed 'in the head'. If additional resources must be taken up in working memory by the computation of (say) 8 x 4, because this number fact is not known very well (is difficult to retrieve from long term memory), then interference and the breakdown of the algorithms or computational procedure is likely to occur. Hence, Resnick and Ford stress the importance of developing number fact knowledge to a high extent, so these facts can be retrieved quickly and easily. This is known as automaticity.

Remediation   The traditional way of developing automaticity is through drill and practice, though this has fallen into disrepute in recent years. However, many, including myself, would recommend the rote learning of tables and mental arithmetic. It is also important to analyse tasks into learning hierarchies, such as that given for arithmetic earlier. Instruction should be based on these hierarchies, giving the appropriate amount of drill and practice.

In their treatment of four dyscalculic adolescents Slade and Russell (1971) found providing copies of multiplication tables resulted in some slight improvement in long multiplication sums. But their biggest success was with one boy who was taught the Trachenberg system (Cutler and McShane, 1962). In this system all basic arithmetic processes are mediated by addition and subtraction.

Atkinson (1983) recommends that remediation should begin with fractions. This has two advantages. First, once the pupils realise that they can handle fractions, 'a major negative barrier is broken' and, secondly they will be handling roughly the same material as normal children. Of course the procedure starts with addition and subtraction, but once they move onto multiplication of fractions, there is a 'natural medium with which to practise multiplication and division facts'. Atkinson admits that it is appropriate at this stage to practice tables in the form of drill and especially the mathematical 'demons' (6 x 3, 6 x 7, 6 x 9, 8 x 7 and 8 x 9). However, the teacher should adopt the practice of teaching through fractions with some caution, as fractions present some difficulty for most children.

Difficulties which arise through a child forgetting to carry correctly may be remedied by using particular calculation methods. For example, in the case of subtraction, using decomposition rather than equal additions as shown below is thought to be a useful method, and one which emphasises the actual mathematical operation.

Methods used in subtraction.

$$
\begin{array}{r}
{}^{\cancel{8}}5 \\
-{}^{5}\cancel{4}7 \\
\hline
38
\end{array}
\qquad
\begin{array}{r}
{}^{7}\cancel{8}5 \\
-\ 47 \\
\hline
38
\end{array}
$$

　　　Equal additions　　　　Decomposition

Setting out computations using expanded notation (e.g. where the number 264 is written out as 200, 60, 4) is also recommended. An example of the use of this in remediation is given later in the chapter.

Spatial Difficulties

Spatial difficulties show themselves when children misalign numbers and fail to maintain place values. Some children also invert or reverse numbers. The problem has sometimes been referred to as spatial dyscalculia (Badian, 1983). Learning difficulties are also seen in the reading of the clock, measuring and geometry.

The problem may be seen in children who do not have an additional reading difficulty (Badian, 1983; Rourke and Finlayson, 1978), though poor readers sometimes have such spatial problems as well (Beech, 1985; Spellacy and Peters, 1978). This specific learning difficulty is sometimes referred to as Developmental Gerstmann Syndrome. The term was first used by Kinsbourne and Warrington (1963) in comparing children with brain damaged adults. The adults usually had brain damage to the parieto-occipital area of the left (dominant) hemisphere. They exhibited a combination of symptoms including right-left disorientation, finger agnosia (inability to discriminate between fingers), agraphia (writing disability) and dyscalculia. However, whether children with spatial problems in mathematics are really comparable to these brain-damaged adults is a matter for debate (Badian, 1983). Also, there would seem to be some confusion to the hemisphere involved in spatial mathematics disability. Some researchers indicate that the right hemisphere is usually involved in spatial ability (Badian, 1983; Rourke and Strang, 1978), but the Gerstmann Syndrome usually involves the left (dominant) hemisphere. Badian also maintains that children with spatial difficulties in mathematics, if they have reading problems at all, will be visual dyslexics. In the area of mathematics, children who have spatial difficulties will be fairly able in the area of computation. Their knowledge of tables and mathematical operations will be relatively good. Spatial difficulties in mathematics may be linked to a deficit in Thurstone's (1938) spatial factor S.

Spatial difficulties are seen in the calculations performed by Ralph, an 11-year-old boy studied by Farnham-Diggory (1978). His mistakes in computation were mainly due to misalignment, as in this example:

```
   23
+   5
   73
```

In the next example, he began writing from the left. He realised his answer was incorrect, so ignored the five, giving 21. This is called a reversal error.

```
   19
+  16
  215
```

In the following subtraction example he subtracted the 15 from the number below, treating it as if it were 70.

```
   15
-   7
   65
```

An example of Joffe's (1980) shows that the problem can occur with more complicated calculations:

```
     236
   x 142
   23600
   94 4 0
    47 2
  968702
```

Another reversal error is seen in this example of Cohn's (1961):

```
    963
    x69
   8751    6 x 3, 6 x 6 etc. written left
   7386    to right reversal and table
  94896    error.
```

Similar reversal errors are seen in the following simple sums given by Badian (1983):

```
    65
    +8
   613
```

```
   52.04
 -  5.30
   47.26
```

Place values are often ignored by children with spatial difficulties in mathematics, as given below (Joffe, 1980):

```
      23
  3) 609    Failure to insert 0
```

In the next example the child fails to keep the decimal point:

```
    2.4
  x  .2
    4.8
```

Problems which have a spatial element were included in the survey of 10-year-olds carried out by Ward (1979). For the problem:

Divide this shape into just four triangles

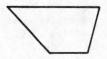

only 54% of the children were correct, 23% giving the answer as

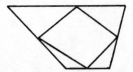

For the problem:

This letter can be cut in half along the axis of symmetry.

Show the axis of symmetry for:

only 45% of the children were correct, 33% giving the answer as

These examples demonstrate that problems of a spatial nature are quite difficult for a 10-year-old child, though misalignment in calculation is relatively uncommon, as Ward's survey does not mention it as a source of error in calculation.

Remediation   Remedial procedures for children with spatial difficulties in general are dealt with in considerable detail in the work of Frostig and Maslow (1973). Kephart (1970) and Johnson and Myklebust (1967). One idea for children with problems in the alighment of numbers is for them to use a cardboard screen to obliterate the irrelevant left-hand column during computation, as shown below for the sum 45 + 24:

```
┌─────────────────┐
│                 │ 5
│     Screen      │
│                 │ 4
└─────────────────┘
```

The use of squared paper might help those with a less serious alignment problem. Also, automatic skills in mental arithmetic can be developed to the extent of relieving the burden on working memory.

Frequently, a child will begin a computation (e.g. addition) at the left instead of the right-hand column, revealing a problem in right-left discrimination. In carrying out a computation correctly, the child has to work ᵢn a different direction from that involved in reading and writing. Young children especially are confused over left and right and training in right-left awareness is necessary. Frostig and Maslow (1973) and Johnson and Myklebust (1967) advise that games such as 'Simon Says' are useful. In this version of 'Simon Says' the child has to respond to instructions like 'Simon says raise your right arm' and the child responds to the command only if preceded by 'Simon says'. There are also various paper and pencil exercises, tracing games, etc., which can assist in the development of body image and right-left orientation (Frostig and Horne, 1973). Materials are also available from Learning Development Aids.

HIGHER ORDER DIFFICULTIES IN MATHEMATICS

Sometimes children's difficulties in mathematics appear to permeate all aspects of the subject. For instance the level of understanding of mathematical concepts may be low, or they may have great difficulty in understanding the language used. In both these cases I would not be referring to specific learning difficulties in mathematics, but would recognise that the learning difficulty is with the grasping of mathematical concepts, a general cognitive deficit, which we will now examine in detail.

Difficulty in Understanding Mathematics

One would have thought that a child's general understanding of mathematics would be related to general intelligence and, indeed, many factor analytic studies of mathematical ability have demonstrated the importance of general intelligence in mathematical performance (Thorndike, 1922; Thurstone, 1938; Werdelin, 1958).

Thorndike, for example, demonstrated a correlation between mathematics and general intelligence ranging from .55 to .70, using different mathematics tests. As mentioned earlier, this general ability is usually designated as factor g.

Throughout the sixties and seventies the importance of mathematical understanding was greatly emphasised. The general rationale being that many children were attempting to carry out mathematical computations without understanding them and thereby often were getting them wrong. There was also the suggestion that in so doing the child would become fixed or set in his or her incorrect ways (Choat, 1980; Cockroft, 1982; Denvir et al, 1982; Ward, 1979). For example, the DES report of 1979 on secondary school mathematics, states 'such a concentration on calculation devoid of application and motivation is often counterproductive'. Denvir et al (1982) give the example of Tim (aged 13 years), who wrote:

$$
\begin{array}{r}
327 \\
\times\ 10 \\
\hline
327 \\
3270 \\
\hline
3597
\end{array}
$$

Denvir concludes that such a result is obtained by a child who has not grasped the nature of the process and states 'this suggests that learning rules without understanding is unlikely to be a reliable strategy'. The view is not without its opponents, however, for example, Levy (1976), who maintained that 'teaching, the use of a process must wait until understanding has been achieved, is dangerous nonsense'.

The theoretical basis for this stress on understanding stemmed from the work of various psychologists, including Piaget (1953), Bruner (1964), Dienes and Jeeves (1965) and Skemp (1971). Their theories are expertly reviewed in many books on mathematics (e.g. Dean, 1982). There is a certain amount of evidence to suggest that the development of mathematical understanding is much slower than formerly thought. Research by Sayer, Kuchemann and Wylam, 1976), for example, has indicated that Piaget's concrete operational stage normally lasts from 7 to 12 years of age, but many 15-year-olds also remain at that level. This would seem to indicate that the higher levels of abstraction (at the formal operational level), which are needed for mathematical thinking, may not be within the reach of many 12- to 15-year-olds, though of course many

9-year-olds are capable of such thinking. The enormous variability in the development of mathematical understanding was also pointed out by Cockcroft (1982) and Denvir et al (1982).

Hart (1981) gave the example of two 12-year-old children who were also slow to develop mathematical thinking. They were asked to choose the correct operation for a problem:

A bucket holds 8 litres of water. Four buckets of water are emptied into a bath. How do you work out how many litres are in the bath?
(Circle one answer.)

$$8 \times 4 \qquad 4 \div 8$$
$$12 - 8 \qquad 8 \div 4$$
$$8 + 4 \qquad 4 \times 8$$
$$4 + 4 \qquad 8 - 4$$

Neither child could do this or similar problems, which would suggest that they had difficulty in relating the numerical operation to the verbal problem and probably remained at Piaget's concrete operational level. This was also indicated by performance on other tests.

Other studies have shown that meaningful learning is more effective than rote learning as it is better remembered and more transferable. In one study carried out by Rae and McPhillimy (1971) children were taught subtraction by decomposition. One group were given a meaningful explanation:

If we subtract 26 from 82, ten is borrowed from the 80, making it 70 and increasing 2 to 12

$$\begin{array}{r} {}^{7}8{}^{1}2 \\ - \ 26 \\ \hline 56 \end{array}$$

The other group were taught a mechanical process. After such instruction the group who were given the meaningful explanation were better on learning and retention and transferred their learning to 3-digit sums easily.

Choat (1980) claims that rote learning is important and that meaningfulness can develop even through rote learning. If children practise tables continuously they come to realise what these tables mean (according to Choat). Such meaningful rote learning, he claims, can occur through bringing existing knowledge to bear on the repetitive rote skill.

Remediation   The   recent   history (in the last twenty
years) has advocated teaching mathematics by encouraging
the child's understanding of the concepts involved. Thus
remedial   teaching   of   mathematics   nowadays   has
understanding as a main focus. What else then is needed
in the remedial treatment of mathematics? First of all
this ethos is a long way from being put into practice.
For example, Denvir et al (1982) advise that smaller
classes and group work will assist in developing greater
understanding.   But more important is the development of
teacher awareness through training.   Especially, the
teacher needs 'more effective ways of identifying the
point at which the pupil fails and suggestions for
appropriate remediation'.   In this chapter I have
stressed careful teacher observation of children's
errors, which should form the basis of remediation.
Unfortunately, we have not yet developed the highly
specific methods of identification and remediation
needed, although the use of learning hierarchies and the
information theory approach to learning mathematics will
help.
     The   following two case studies are given to
demonstrate the usefulness of two different approaches to
remediation.   The first is what might be termed a
'learning through understanding' approach and the second
an 'information theory approach'. In fact both provide
the children with routes to understanding which are
different from the routes they have failed with.
     Magné (1978) gives the case of Helen who has
difficulty in reading and writing 2- or 3- digit numbers.
For her, remedial procedures using blocks proved
successful, in order for her to develop an understanding
of the order of digits in writing numbers. The case also
illustrates that it is important that the child
internalises mathematical operations.   To quote from
Magné:

     'Helen was late in grasping the meaning of letters
     and numbers. At the age of nine she got a few weekly
     hours of remedial teaching. Helen did not understand
     how to write 2- or 3- digit numbers. We let her use
     a set of blocks (Dienes blocks) which we have found
     most   useful   for   getting   low-achieving   or
     underachieving children to learn the number system.
         Helen used these blocks with her exercises. To
     begin with it appeared nearly impossible for her to
     realise the meaning of the numbers. Nor did she seem
     able to see the significance of the material. But an

132

improvement was on it's way. At first Helen succeeded in producing the correct number of blocks, when the teacher had, for example, instructed her to represent the number 207, or to tell the number 207, when the teacher laid the blocks in front of her.

For a long time Helen could only work with the help of the blocks. But one day she achieved a dramatic triumph. Helen said to her teacher 'I need no blocks. Because, when I write 207, I have two flats and seven cubes inside my head and no longs at all. And so, you see Miss, it is 207'.

The second case is that of Resnick and Ford's (1981) child Leslie, aged 9 years. Leslie used a faulty subtraction rule (or algorithm). The faulty rule was that the smaller number should be subtracted from the larger number regardless of it's position. Leslie knew something about place value from her work in addition, where she always carried numbers correctly. When shown the following two sums:

$$36 \qquad 27$$
$$-27 \qquad -36$$

Leslie claimed that they were identical.

In terms of the learning hierarchy for subtraction of Gagné and Briggs (1974), shown in Figure 6.2, Leslie had proceeded, with some difficulty, to level 4. The next step in the hierarchy was to learn to subtract with borrowing. This was carried out, using Dienes blocks, as shown in Figure 6.3. The subtraction procedure was demonstrated to Leslie using these blocks and then Leslie was given a series of sums to answer using the blocks. Within 40 minutes Leslie was answering all sums correctly without hesitation, including problems with zeros. The blocks were 'faded out' and in a further 10 minutes Leslie was solving written problems correctly.

Resnick and Ford claimed that there was strong evidence that Leslie now understood the whole subtraction algorithm, and to test this she was seen three weeks later. On this occasion she was given a brief explanation of expanded notation. The first problem Leslie was given was:

$$700$$
$$-356$$

Leslie completed the sum thus:

Figure 6.3: Sample of the procedure used to train Leslie in subtraction using Dienes blocks (Resnick and Ford, 1981)

TRAINING PROCEDURE	DIENES BLOCKS REPRESENTATION	
	Tens	Units
For the problem $\begin{array}{r} 85 \\ -\,47 \end{array}$ 1. Represent the 85 with blocks.		
2. Start in the ones column and try to remove the 7 blocks shown in the subtrahend. 3. There aren't enough blocks there, so go to the tens column and "borrow" a ten-bar. 4. On the written problem, cross out the 8 and write 7, to show the change in blocks in the tens column. $\begin{array}{r} {}^{7}\!\!\not{8}5 \\ -\,47 \end{array}$		
5. Trade the ten-bar for 10 ones-cubes and place them in the ones column. 6. On the written problem, represent this by writing a 1 that changes the 5 to 15: $\begin{array}{r} {}^{7}\!\!\not{8}\not{5} \\ -\,47 \end{array}$		
7. Now remove the number of blocks shown in the ones column of the subtrahend. 8. Count the number of ones blocks remaining, and write the answer in the ones column of the written problem: $\begin{array}{r} {}^{7}\,{}^{1}\!\!\not{8}\not{5} \\ -\,47 \\ \hline 8 \end{array}$		
9. Go to the tens column and try to remove the number of blocks shown in the subtrahend. 10. Since there are enough blocks, complete the operation, count the blocks remaining and write the answer in the tens column of the written problem: $\begin{array}{r} {}^{7}\,{}^{1}\!\!\not{8}\not{5} \\ -\,47 \\ \hline 38 \end{array}$		

L: Writes: 700 + 00 + 0
          300 + 50 + 6
'I have to go here (hundreds column) 'cause there's nothing to borrow from here (tens column).'

E: 'You are borrowing a hundred from here (the 700). Where are you going to move it to?'

L: 'Here (points to the zero in the ones column).'

E: 'If you move it here this (the zero) becomes a hundred. Then 6 from 100 would have to be what?'

L: 'Ninety-four'.

E: 'How will you write that?'

L: Writes the 4 in the ones column. Changes the 00 in the tens column to 90, thus:

$$\begin{array}{ccc} 600 & 9 & \\ \cancel{700} + \cancel{00} + {}_{10}0 \\ 300 + 50 + 6 \\ & & 4 \end{array}$$

Resnick and Ford suggested that such a success with a child after only three weeks was due to a new method which tapped her already considerable knowledge. 'We conjecture that the instruction linked the written subtraction algorithm to place value knowledge Leslie already possessed.' If remediation can help children to realise that they actually have some knowledge and ability in mathematics it will go a long way to alleviate anxiety and to encourage mathematical self-esteem, which as we shall see is a very important factor in mathematical achievement.

Difficulties with the Language of Mathematics

Mathematical terms are often confused or misunderstood. This would seem to occur more often in children with reading difficulties than in those without. In a study by Joffe (1980) 50% of children with reading difficulties were stuck when asked to find the total of two numbers, and this after having done eight addition sums correctly. They did not grasp the meaning of the word 'total'. The difficulty is seen mostly in mathematical problem-solving, especially where there is no clue as to the mathematical operation to be performed. For example, take the problem:

'If Fred, Alan and John have 33 marbles altogether and each has an equal share, how many does John have?'

Many children failed to see that this was a division problem.

Wheeler and McNutt (1982) have made a systematic study of the effect of language development on children's ability to solve mathematical word problems. They gave low achieving 11-year-olds sets of word problems graded for three levels of difficulty in sentence structure (easy, moderate and hard). The problems themselves were at the same level of mathematical complexity. The children could do many more of the easy and moderate problems than the difficult problems. An example of an easy problem is:

> Jim likes to bake cookies for his family. Last night he baked 50 cookies. He gave 24 of them to a friend. How many cookies will his family have to eat?'

An example of a hard problem is:

> If it is 23 miles on bicycle from Jim's home to Bob's home by staying on the streets and it is 15 miles shorter by cutting through the park, how long is the trip the shorter way?'

Hard problems are those that contain either a compound sentence and a complex interrogative sentence or a compound/complex interrogative sentence (as in the example above). There is an advantage in giving easy problems that contain simple sentences, where the computation required is obvious, when teaching children with learning difficulties. Problems of increasing difficulty should be introduced gradually and the wording discussed with their introduction. It may also be important to limit vocabulary.

FURTHER ISSUES IN MATHEMATICS EDUCATION

So far I have not discussed two issues which, for some researchers, are central to any discussion of difficulties in mathematics. These are the reasons for the superior mathematical achievement of boys, when compared with girls, and emotional factors affecting achievement.

Sex differences in Mathematical Ability

Various surveys (Foxman et al, 1978, 1980; Shuard, 1982) have demonstrated boys' superior achievement to girls in the area of mathematics. The reasons for this sex difference has been hotly debated (Beckwith and Woodruff, 1983; Benbow, 1983). There are those who propose that a genetic visuospatial factor is responsible for the superior performance of boys (Broverman et al, 1968; Buffery and Gray, 1972). Others maintain that social conditioning leads to loss of interest and confidence in mathematics in girls (Badger, 1981; Fennema, 1974).

Yet the sex differences in mathematical achievement are by no means clear cut. These would seem to vary according to the ages of the children being studied and the type of mathematics being tested. In the surveys carried out by Foxman et al (1978, 1980) it was demonstrated that, whereas there was a sex difference in mathematical achievement in the 15-year-olds studied, there was no overall sex difference in the younger children. This is because deficiencies in one area are balanced by ability in another. The differences that were found in the 11-year-olds seem to be in the area of measurement, money, time, weight, decimals, fractions and spatial abilities. Girls were actually superior in the area of computation at age 11. Similar differences were reported by Ward (1979) in a study of ten-year-old children. Girls were better than boys in 11 out of 91 items, which mostly involved making deductions from verbal information. Boys were better than girls in 14 out of 91 items mostly where these involved place value and equations. In older boys (15-year-olds) the superior achievement is in the area of mathematical reasoning, algebra and geometry. The picture that emerges is that boys are better at some aspects of mathematics and girls at other aspects, at least as far as primary school children are concerned. As children get older boys tend to develop superiority in two areas (Badger, 1981). These are spatial ability and problem solving.

Prior to the 1950s it was popular to attribute these differences to innate differences in mathematical ability. Later, it was thought that mathematical ability in boys might be due to their superior spatial ability (Buffery and Gray, 1972; Werdelin, 1958). This even led to popularisation in the concept of a mathematics gene (Purden-Smith and De Severe, 1982).

Lately, there has been a shift in opinion in favour of an environmentalist explanation for sex differences in mathematics. The fact that the mathematical deficiency in girls only really appears from age 11 is seen as an indication that social factors are responsible. Girls lack motivation in the area of mathematics, which is thought to be due to lack of encouragement by parents, teachers and others (Milton, 1959). Another popular idea is that girls become more and more anxious about their mathematical ability (Brush, 1979), devalue and underestimate their performance and hence develop low self-esteem and a less than positive attitude towards mathematics (Fennema, 1979). Prowess in mathematics is not part of a girl's self-image as she is socialised towards the more feminine pursuits of art and literature. Mathematics is seen as a male subject (Nash, 1978). Fennema (1979) also mentions another environmental factor in that girls in secondary school actively spend less time doing mathematics than boys, as they do not usually study the mathematics related subjects such as physics and geometrical drawing to the same extent as boys.

There has been much heated debate about the reasons for sex differences in mathematics. This led Benbow (1983) to claim 'It seems likely that putting every faith in boy and girl socialisation processes as the only permissible explanation of sex differences in mathematical reasoning is premature.' The reasoning behind this statement was that if mathematical difficulty in girls is totally environmentally caused then all areas of mathematics would be affected (including computation) and not just spatial factors and mathematical reasoning. A further viewpoint is given by Badger (1981), who came to the conclusion that spatial and other innate factors might affect mathematical performance in boys, but 'attitudes rooted in the cultural milieu and reinforced by society are probably the determining factor as to whether or not girls succeed in mathematics.'

Emotional Factors and Mathematical Difficulties

As mentioned before, Schonell (1937) thought that backwardness in arithmetic was due as much to emotional as to intellectual factors. He saw that an early failure might have a cumulative effect in that it produces anxiety which might effect the next stage of learning. Mathematics and arithmetic are subjects which have a hierarchical structure, where new skills are built upon the old and would be particularly susceptible to the effects of anxiety because of this. The view is restated in the work of Skemp (1971) and Cockcroft (1982). Loss of self-esteem, confidence and concentration results and is thought to be responsible for lack of progress in mathematics, particularly in girls.

Schonell thought that unevenness in attainment and variation in performance on tests indicated that anxiety was a problem. Such variability suggests that a child is capable in some areas where he or she has been able to concentrate, but not in others where anxiety has prevented learning. He quotes the case of Kathleen (aged 12:5 years), who had an arithmetic age of only 9:5 years. Attainment in the area of mathematical problems was particularly poor and Kathleen made the mistakes as shown below:

$$\begin{array}{r} 12 \\ 34+ \\ 23 \\ \hline 68 \end{array}$$

$$\begin{array}{r} 588 \\ \hline 4\,)\,2344 \end{array}$$

However, Kathleen was successful with two apparently more difficult computations.

$$\begin{array}{r} 7527.4 \\ -\ 3698.6 \\ \hline 3838.8 \end{array}$$

$$\begin{array}{r} 5860.3 \\ \hline 15\,)\,879045 \end{array}$$

This illustrates the unevenness in Kathleen's performance. Schonell states that Kathleen's reactions fluctuated between anxiety and apathy and she had developed the habit of daydreaming.

Skemp (1971) cites the Yerkes-Dodson Law of 1908 to demonstrate the relationship between anxiety and performance. There is a curvilinear relationship between the two, which has been demonstrated in such disparate situations as the adult performance on a perceptual task and rats running a maze. The peak of the curve (optimal performance) occurs at high levels of anxiety for a simple task and at low levels of anxiety for a difficult task (Figure 6.4). If mathematics is thought of as a difficult task, as it is for many, then even slight anxiety can be detrimental to performance.

Figure 6.4: Diagramatic representations of the Yerkes-Dodson Law

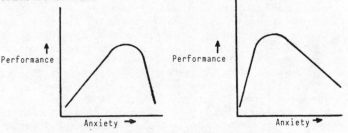

Anxiety and performance on an easy task.

Anxiety and performance on a difficult task.

Anxiety about mathematics continues into adult life. This point was stressed by Cockcroft (1982) in a survey of adults' attitudes to mathematics. Half the people approached refused to be questioned on the subject and when asked why, they referred to discomfort, anxiety and even panic concerning the subject.

SUMMARY

Although we can give many examples of the types of errors children make when doing mathematics, we are at the beginning of a long path as far as effective diagnosis and remediation is concerned. At present mathematical tests, whilst giving a good assessment of a child's ability over the whole subject of mathematics, do not provide for the detailed analysis of errors, which is necessary for effective remediation.

The remedial methods which have been recommended are likewise based on scant research and even heresay. There are very few studies which have properly employed control groups to ascertain whether one method is better than another. Most of the research has been in the area of learning through understanding versus learning by rote and, whilst good of its kind, this research is limited as far as the remediation of learning difficulties in mathematics are concerned.

The personal and social development of children used to
be considered to be mainly under the influence of
parental upbringing and other environmental determinants.
It was not until Johnson and Myklebust's (1967) work that
difficulties in this area were seen as learning
difficulties that might have constitutional origins. The
kind of learning difficulties that are being referred to
are wide ranging but would fall under the umbrella term
of social imperception which Johnson and Myklebust (1967)
define as 'primarily the child's lack of ability to
understand his social environment in terms of his own
behaviour'.

The classification, diagnosis and remediation of
such problems is still in its infancy. They were not
even given a mention in Farnham-Diggory's (1978) book on
the subject. Nevertheless it is extremely important that
such difficulties are diagnosed and treated as unskilled
children will only develop into unskilled adults. But
what are these children like? Of course they manifest a
variety of difficulties and no two children are alike,
but Myklebust (1975) describes the behaviour of one child
Bill as follows:

> Bill was first identified by his maths teacher;
> other teachers had described him as being unable to
> find his way, especially during the first weeks of
> school; he could not find his way around the
> building, often being on the wrong floor and unable
> to find his seat in the classroom. Once he took
> the teacher's seat so he was the butt of ridicule.
> The P.E. teacher reported that, not knowing where
> he was, he would dress in the hall rather than in
> the locker room. Moreover, he was unable to learn
> the combination of his locker. Having no
> comprehension of time, he would imitate other
> students to get to his classes. Upon arrival in
> the classroom he scanned the faces of other
> students to ascertain whether he was in the right
> class. Bill's learning problem was especially
> evident in maths; he could not compute problems in
> the right-left orientation. He seemed to gain cues
> from verbal instructions but not from visual
> presentations alone.

This child's problems appeared to be mainly in the area of his self-concept of viewing himself as distinct from others and other objects. Other children's problems seem to be more in the area of social awareness. Yet it is likely that there the abilities are intertwined in development. This is shown in a study by Shantz (1975) who has traced the development of social cognition in children. It is useful to know just what constitutes normal development in order to be able to say whether a child is abnormal in this regard.

Shantz traces four phases in development which coincide with children's stages of cognitive development. The pre-school child with classical egocentricity can identify certain simple emotions from facial cues and can make a judgement as to whether a situation is familiar or not. In the second phase, children between five and seven years of age recognise that another child might have a different perspective. They begin to recognise that an object might look differently from a different position. This is related to the development of body image on oneself and another person. In the area of socialisation at this age children can make inferences about others and there is the beginning of the understanding that another person can have a different thought. But the child is often inaccurate in the thoughts he thinks other people have.

Around the ages of eight or nine most children develop dramatically. They begin to understand that other people can observe and reflect the thoughts and feelings he or she might be having. He or she can look at another viewpoint in greater detail both in terms of spatial understanding and the understanding of social relationships. The child begins to infer the feelings of others when they are in unfamiliar situations.

The fourth phase develops during adolescence. His or her perspective increases to include the self, another person and a third party, the relationships between them and their inner experiences. There is a movement towards explaining thoughts and feelings and not just describing them.

Gottman (1983) has established that several abilities are necessary for the development of friendships between individual children aged between three and nine years of age. Apart from the ability to see another's viewpoint there are other skills such as clarity in communication, information exchange, the establishment of common ground activity and self-disclosure. But there is also the ability to resolve negative aspects such as the exploration of differences (and similarities), the resolution of conflict and so on. Most of these skills develop during play. Often this is accompanied by warm feelings but at other times hostility and conflict predominates. But these negative aspects diminish in the amount of time they take up. In looking at children who did and did not 'hit it off' with a stranger, Gottman found that the child who 'hit it off' was more likely to be clear in the messages he or she was conveying to establish points of similarity, to make weak demands and to use humour. Children who did not 'hit it off' were deficient in these skills and often made strong demands of the other child. Gottman supported the social skills-deficit hypothesis, that is that children who are poor at making friends are deficient in social skills.

THE CLASSIFICATION OF SOCIAL SKILLS PROBLEMS

We have little idea of just how many children are affected in terms of their social skills. As with other learning difficulties, an examination of theories of causation may assist. One model of such learning difficulties is given by Myklebust (1975) and Badian (1983). They point to the fact that many more boys than girls have difficulty with social perception and that it is often associated with mathematical difficulty. Myklebust (1975) reasons:

> It appears that boys are more dependant on non-verbal (right hemisphere) functions and so are superior in this cognitive function. But girls are more dependant on verbal-cognitive (left hemisphere) processes and thus are superior in this type of cognitive function. Therefore boys might sustain a greater handicap than girls in non-verbal learning difficulties.

However, if we adopt this line of reasoning one would expect girls to suffer from difficulties with left hemisphere skills (i.e. speech and language) to a greater extent. But this is not the case.

The second line of reasoning concerning such social problems comes from Torgesen (1977). He argues that learning disabled children are quite inactive. They are unaware of the demands of a task and in other ways show a lack of metacognitive awareness. The same psychological processes underlie a child's performance in both the private and interpersonal situations. Children with learning disabilities, because they are inactive learners, do not consciously monitor the behaviour of others. They are less able to step outside their own experiences and adapt their own behaviour to the behaviour of others.

A third line of argument would focus on the effect of being a learning disabled child. The child will realise that he is quite a failure in the academic sphere which leads to task anxiety. This effect has been discussed at some length in the area of mathematics when such effects are quite dramatic. Such anxiety and lowering of self-esteem will have the effect of making the learning disabled child withdraw from the company of others. In addition negative feedback from other children (in terms of name calling and ostrasization) will have the effect of him interacting less with other children. Through lack of practise he then becomes less able to cope with social interactions.

Myklebust (1975) divided social awareness problems into two main areas. Though a child might have difficulty in both of these they will be covered in turn. The areas are:

1. Self perception
2. Social perception

DIFFICULTY WITH THE PERCEPTION OF SELF

Defined as 'a facet of social perception' (Myklebust, 1975) a child with a disability in this area might have a gross problem with the perception of body image or a minor problem such as finger agnosia.

Difficulty with the perception of body image might be severe in that a child may not recognise his own face or the faces of others. This difficulty is sometimes seen in brain damaged patients (Ellis, 1982) and of course leads to gross problems in relating to other people. Less severe difficulties are those of right-left orientation in space, and right-left recognition on oneself and other people. The child, Bill, described by Myklebust, could identify his own right and left hands but could not identify these on another person. Some children have problems with spatial orientation and might lose their way easily when walking round school.

A less severe problem is that of finger agnosia, again a difficulty which is seen in brain damaged adults, especially those exhibiting Gerstmann's syndrome resulting from brain damage to the left parietal region. In finger agnosia the child has difficulty identifying fingers, for example when blindfolded he or she may be unable to say which fingers are being touched.

These difficulties can be assessed by observation or by applying one or two simple tests. One test which arises from Piaget's work involves the identification of right and left body parts on oneself and another. Most six-year-olds are able to identify right and left on themselves and another person and by the age of eight should be able to execute crossed commands, (e.g. the identification of the right foot with the left hand). Finger agnosia can be tested by the method developed by Kinsbourne and Warrington (1966). The child is asked to close his eyes and asked 'How many fingers am I touching, one or two?' Various combinations of fingers are touched and most six year old children perform at ceiling level on this test. An alternative form is the 'in-between test' where the examiner asks 'How many fingers are there in-between?' Again most children would get most of these correct.

<u>Remediation</u> Methods of treatment for defects in the perception of body image have been recommended for some time. The exercises involve both gross body image and finer aspects. For gross body image various games and exercises are recommended (Kephart, 1970; Frostig and Maslow, 1973). One such exercise is called 'Angels in the snow'. In this children have to lie flat on their backs and perform various tasks, e.g. 'Bring your left leg up and over to touch your right arm.' Other games such as 'Simon Says' can also be useful. Many kits have been produced which provide exercises in body awareness. These range from drawing in missing parts, copying the positions exhibited in a drawing, to doing more and more intricate jigsaw puzzles. Some of these exercises are provided in the Frostig Programme and others by kits supplied by Learning Development Aids.

As with other learning difficulties, the remediation of problems with body image and right-left awareness has not been actively tested. These recommendations are given utmost adequate knowledge as to their usefulness.

DIFFICULTY WITH SOCIAL PERCEPTION

Social perception is quite difficult to assess. Autistic children have more severe problems, and tend to treat adults as objects. This severe psychotic behaviour is not one we shall look at here. Children having difficulties with social perception are described as being poor in independant activities, poor in judging people's emotions and attitudes, insensitive in social situations and doing and saying inappropriate things (Lerner, 1971). One child, Doris, described by Myklebust, exhibited such problems. She was able to relate to her parents emotionally and was reasonably talkative. But she could not relate to persons of her own age, appearing awkward and uncertain as she could not understand what was happening. Many aspects of social relationships are non-verbal and consist in the interpretation of facial expressions, gestures etcetera.

One important piece of research into the social disabilities of these children was carried out by Wong and Wong (1980). Learning-disabled and normal children were asked to look at three cartoon series where the main character displayed an emotion (anger, fear or sadness) after being caught up in a chain of events. For example, in the first cartoon 'Anger' the little boy knocked down a castle of cards which his brother was showing him. The little boy who vented his anger had previously had his sandcastle knocked down and this caused his angry feelings. So the second little boy, the brother, was in a sense an innocent bystander as he had no knowledge of this cause. The child observing this cartoon had to retell the story first of all from the point of view of the main character and then from the point of view of the bystander. In so doing the experimenter gained some measure of the extent to which the child could set aside story details known only to him or herself and adopt a different viewpoint. The results showed that the learning-disabled children were much less able to adopt an alternative viewpoint than their peers. In other words the children were more egocentric, and displayed a lack of awareness of different interpretations of the same event.

Learning-disabled children are not as popular with their peer group as other children. This can be studied using sociograms. One such sociogram for a group of children in a special class is given in Figure 7.1. In this study children were asked to make three choices (the child they would choose first, second and third) in each of three areas, i.e. the child they would like to play with in the playground, the child they would most like to sit next to and the child they would like to take home for tea. As can be seen from Figure 7.1, the child who was one of the least popular, child 6, had least friendship choices, was rated as maladjusted by the Bristol Social Adjustment Guide.

In a series of studies by Bryan (1974, 1976, 1978) various characteristics of learning-disabled children

Figure 7.1: Sociogram depicting friendship choices for
10 subjects in a special class in an ordinary primary
school. (First choices only depicted.)
(From Harding and McLaughan, 1985)

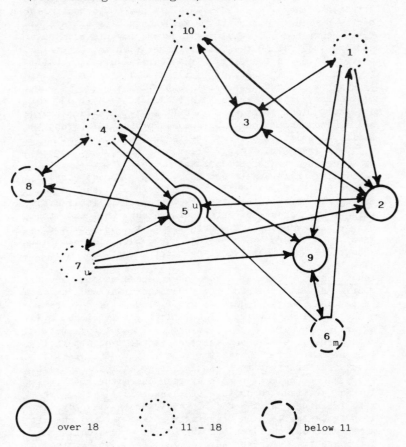

over 18   11 – 18   below 11

were in evidence. They interacted less with teachers and peers and if they initiated a conversation they were twice as likely as normal children to be ignored. In several sociometric analyses children were asked such questions as 'Who is (and who is not) your friend?' and 'Who is worried or scared?'. Again the learning-disabled children were not chosen as friends and were described by others as scared, unhappy and worried. A laboratory study showed that learning-disabled children made more seemingly helpful on task statements, but these were seen as meddlesome by the other children. In a study on altruism they donated more money (payment for participation) to a charity even when not being watched. This increased altruism and generosity is seen as an attempt to repair their self-image after the experience of rejection on the part of the learning-disabled child. A further study (Bryan, 1978) involved the children in picking the most appropriate label for a piece of film. Of course, the learning-disabled children found this difficult indicating again a difficulty in understanding social communications. Wiig and Harris (1974) reported similar results with learning-disabled adolescents.

In summary, these difficulties seem to be a result of incorrect interpretation of social interactions. In particular non-verbal communications are not correctly understood. This results in the learning-disabled child making inappropriate attempts at social interaction, being too generous, offering help which is misunderstood, but withdrawing to a certain extent from interaction. This results in them being unpopular, less socially acceptable and probably quite unhappy.

Remediation   Several researchers have made a plea for social skills training in learning-disabled children (Wong and Wong, 1980; Minskoff, 1980). Ten years ago such training involved role playing exercises. For example, Chandler (1973) trained delinquent boys between the ages of eleven and thirteen years, over a period of ten weeks. They had to role play various real life events alternating their acting roles so that each child had the opportunity to play each character. They also looked at video recordings of these role plays to assist the training. At the end of this exercise the boys were less egocentric. Such training was also carried out with nursery school children. Staub (1971) placed children in four groups. These were: role playing in helping and being helped; induction training in which the experimenter pointed out the consequences of helping; combined role play and induction training; and a control group. For boys the combined role play and induction training was the most effective, whereas for girls role playing alone was effective. In the role play situation the child had to play the role of another child who needed to be helped, but an element of reinforcement by the adult approving of them was also apparent.

Other researchers (Fry, 1969; Shantz and Wilson, 1972) have attempted to help the child take the role of the listener in communication. In these studies children had to talk about various designs and discuss the adequacy of the message from the listener's point of view. Communicative ability increased in the children studied.

More recently Minskoff (1980) has described a more systematic approach based on the task analysis of non-verbal communication skills into step-by-step teaching sequences. Specifically, the areas of non-verbal communication which are analysed were

    i)   Facial expressions

    ii) Gestures

    iii) Postures

The section on postures involved four areas, the descrimination of postures, understanding the social meaning of postures, the meaningful usage of postures and applying postural cues to communication situations.

Some of the teaching was by direct interpretation of body language. To teach the discrimination of postures the teacher showed the children pictures and videos of unlike postures and they discussed similarities and differences, emotions portrayed and so on with some imitation. Later more similar postures were discussed. For example, fatigue versus energetic, were discussed first as the postures are quite dissimilar. Later postures such as anger, fear and worry were discussed, as these appear quite similar.

In the section on applying postural cues the children role played situations. In doing so they analysed the postures and their effects on other people. They could project the consequences of using inappropriate postures, e.g. the consequences of disinterest when trying for a basketball team. They also had to interpret inconsistent cues and rely on the non-verbal message more than the verbal message, for example the child might have said 'I love insects', but showed a posture of dislike by holding the body back. They might also have demonstrated an inconsistent facial grimace.

These studies demonstrate that role playing and other techniques can assist in the social development of learning-disabled children. But some more careful research is necessary to discover just which factors are important, especially as Shantz (1975) comments that there is as many negative studies as there are positive ones.

SUMMARY

The ability to make friends and to differentiate between strangers and friends is crucial for survival and emotional happiness. Learning disabilities in this area have only recently been acknowledged. In early life the child may not respond appropriately to friends and strangers and will fail to pick up valuable social cues. They may have difficulty in the perception of body image, discriminating themselves from others and especially in discriminating left from right. Later as he or she goes to school the child with learning disablities in this area will respond inappropriately to others as he or she fails to develop social perception. Such a child is quite likely to have difficulty in mathematics. The long range prospect is a lifestyle with few friends, a limited range of activities and possibly no work. Fortunately now such problems are being recognised such difficulties may be remedied. Especially useful in this area is the use of role play and video camera work in social skills training in children.

8. A WAY FORWARD

In this survey of learning disabilities and their remediation one theme is dominant. In each of the specified areas there are several types of learning disability. There is not just one type of reading problem or spelling problem but many. A second rather disconcerting point follows from this observation. The classification of learning disabilities in each of the specified areas is given only tentatively. Research into learning disabilities has not yet reached the point where categorical classifications can be given. It follows then that many of the remedial techniques that are advised are based on scanty knowledge. Research into the effectiveness of the advised techniques is also sadly lacking.

However in the last ten years there have been changes in the way researchers think about learning difficulties and the basis for them. In the first chapter I outlined a model of learning disabilities which helped us to think more clearly, that is, the clinical model of the Illinois Test of Psycholinguistic Abilities. With its emphasis on psychological processes this gave us some insight into the characteristics of learning disabilities. An additional approach which also gives information is the neurological examination of brain-damaged patients. These two approaches, the examination of cognitive processes and research into brain-damaged patients, have been fundamental in the development of a branch of psychology known as cognitive psychology.

According to Humphreys (1985) cognitive psychology attempts to answer specific questions, such as 'What processes do we need to go through in order to perform a certain task (e.g. reading a word)?' A model or flow diagram is produced which illustrates the various processes involved which can then be tested empirically. An example of such a model is given by Ellis (1984) to explain the processes involved in the recognition of a heard word. A person hears the spoken word and then analyses the word acoustically. The word is then looked for in the word store and some kind of word recognition takes place, and then the meaning of the word is understood. If the word is written down an additional process takes place. We can all answer such questions as

'Is a phoks an animal?' or 'Can you sail a yott?'. This is because we translate the visual impression of the graphemes (letter groups) to phonemes (sounds) and then blend these together to make a word. These two routes involved in word recognition are represented diagrammatically in Figure 8.1.

Figure 8.1: Information processing diagram to represent some processes involved in the recognition of a word (after Ellis, 1984)

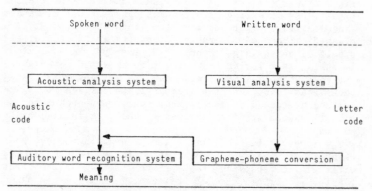

Such an analysis is very useful because it implies that there are several stages between a stimulus and a response. Each stage is dependent on a previous stage and each of these processes or stages takes time. The different models can be tested by experimentation or by references to brain damaged patients who may have some processes intact whilst others are changed. Coltheart (1985) has explored brain-damaged patients in order to understand the processes involved in adult readers. This has helped us to understand the processes involved in going from print to meaning, for example. These same processes are relevant to children with reading disabilities. Two explanations are popular. In the first explanation the person sees the printed word and instantly recognises the meaning and then he says it. In the second explanation the person says over the word in his (or her) head and then recognises its meaning. We know this second explanation cannot be true because of the recognition of homophones. For example, we can distinguish between 'sale' and 'sail' or 'blew' and 'blue'. And yet the first explanation cannot be entirely correct either. This is because there are patients with deep dyslexia who can read aloud irregular words such as 'shoe', 'sew' and 'word' but who cannot explain what these words mean. Coltheart carried out a number of experiments with this and other patients and concluded that most people can use both methods of processing. Both of the explanations given are thought to be correct, and that a person switches from one mode of processing to another. In carrying out experiments it is possible to sort out these problems in greater detail.

In one experiment (Coltheart, 1985) the patient was found to be able to pick out the picture that corresponded to the written word 'brush'. This was easy when the picture was amongst unlike pictures (for example, a picture of a brush and a picture of a cup). However, the patient found the task difficult if the picture of the brush appeared with a similar picture (for example, a picture of a comb). This experiment demonstrates that the patient was confused about meaning. Brush and comb are similar in meaning because they fulfil the same function. This also occurred when the words were given in spoken form. So it is likely that visual pictures can use the same meaning route as spoken words. These proceses are given in Figure 8.2.

Figure 8.2: Processes involved in the recognition of words, and objects.

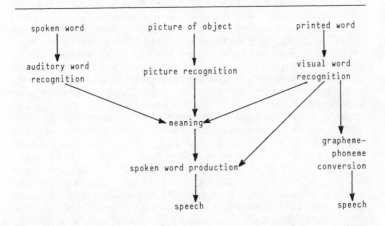

This research now gives us a better idea of the processes involved in reading, language and picture recognition. It is not a complete account and cognitive psychologists have produced quite elaborate diagrams to explain the processes more fully. The reader is referred to Ellis (1984) and Patterson and Shewell (1986) for this. However, the example does serve to illustrate a couple of points. Firstly, if the processes are analysed carefully this will give some insight into the processes involved in learning disabilities. In the sphere of reading it seems likely that there are several routes involved in going from print through meaning to speech. The whole word to meaning route and the grapheme-phoneme correspondence route are two obviously different routes. Difficulties can occur at any point in the route from print to speech. Not all the processes have been reproduced here so it seems likely that several types of learning difficulty would occur. Ellis (1984) describes possible forms of developmental dyslexia which in part are similar to dyslexias occurring in adults. These are, developmental deep dyslexia, developmental surface dyslexia, developmental letter by letter (spelling) dyslexia and developmental phonemic dyslexia.

Secondly, if the processes are analysed correctly this will give predictions for remediation. For example, a child with problems in grapheme-phoneme conversion will be able to compensate by using an alternative route in remediation. This is the old tried method of compensation for the weaknesses by using the child's strengths. There is the added advantage that a detailed description of the specific processes will yield specific remedial recommendations.

It should also be apparent that some processes are separate from one another. Ellis makes the point that spelling errors should be analysed separately from reading errors and gives the example of a person of seventeen years of age who was poor at phonic reading, but good at phonic spelling. In spelling she mainly gave words which were like the required word in sound (e.g. 'solom' for 'solemn', 'matres' for 'mattress'). She spelt regular words such as 'chair' better than irregular words such as 'yacht'. However, in reading this person would be able to read more common words such as 'of', 'the', 'man' with little difficulty but could not break common words into sounds. This is because different processes are involved in reading and spelling although there are also some common processes.

Specifically, two routes are involved in spelling, the auditory route and the visual-motor route. In reading the input or receptive process is being used in the main (going from print to meaning) and in spelling the output part of the system (going from meaning to print). This is represented in Figure 8.3.

The routes involved in reading are firstly the grapheme-phoneme conversion route, to phonemic output to speech (marked 'a' in Figure 8.3). This allows for a child to be able to read a word without understanding its

Figure 8.3: Diagram to illustrate the processes involved in reading and spelling (based on Ellis, 1984 and Patterson and Shewell, 1986)

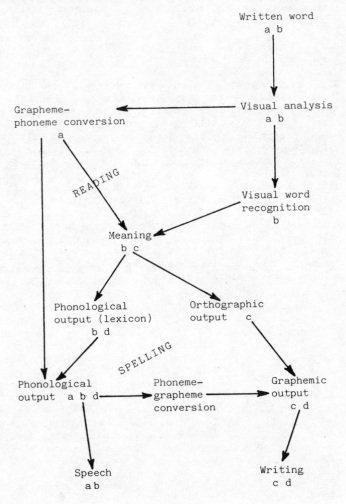

meaning, though meaning can be accessed. The same initial route is used in visual whole word recognition but meaning is accessed directly and the reader moves to phonological output and speech (marked 'b' in Figure 8.3). A child who is trying to spell a word can go straight from meaning to the visual representation (as in 'c'), or via a phoneme-grapheme correspondence route to sound (marked 'd'). So we can see that the routes and processes involved in reading and spelling overlap very little and the child may be using completely different pathways in each.

CONCLUSION

So, when we are looking at the specific learning difficulties a child may have, it would be as well to analyse the processes involved in a given task quite carefully. This will then lead to specific remedial recommendations. This does not discredit all the valuable work which has been described in this book. It is quite likely that much that has been found to be useful, in the VAKT method for example, will fit into this analysis. Research that has concentrated on different types of learning difficulty (Orton's work, for example) should also concur with these processes. The introduction of cognitive psychology into this field may only serve to legitimise certain classifications and techniques. Hopefully it will also serve to stimulate research into the learning processes involved which can only help the children involved.

REFERENCES

Andrews, G. and Harris, M. (1964). The syndrome of
    stuttering. London: Spastics Society Medical
    Education and Information Unit.
Arnheim, D. and Sinclair, W. (1975). The clumsy child.
    Saint Louis: Mosby.
Atkinson, B. (1983). Arithmetic remediation and the
    learning disabled adolescent: Fractions and
    interest level. Journal of Learning Disabilities,
    16, 403 - 406.
Badger, M. E. (1981). Why aren't girls better at maths?
    A review of research. Educational Research, 24, 11
    - 23.
Badian, N. A. (1983). Dyscalculia and non verbal
    disorders of learning. In Myklebust, H. Progress
    in learning disabilities, 5, 235 - 264. New York:
    Grune and Stratton.
Bailey, T. (1978). Learning problems - how to cope.
    Forward Trends, 5, (4), 10.
Bantock, G. H. (1980). Dilemmas of the curriculum.
    Martin Robertson.
Barton, A. H. (1963). Reading research and its
    communication. The Columbia-Carnegie project. In
    Figurel J.A. (ed.), Reading as an intellectual
    activity. Newark, Del: IRA.
Bateman, B. (1966). In Hellmuth, J., Learning
    disorders, 2. Seattle Child Publications.
Battle, E. S. and Lacey, B. (1972). A context for
    hyperactivity in children over time. Child
    Development, 43, 757 - 773.
Beckwith, J. and Woodruff, M. (1983). Achievement in
    mathematics (letter). Science, 223, 1247.
Beech, J. R. (1983). The effects of spelling change on
    the adult reader. Spelling Progress Bulletin, 13,
    11 - 18.
Beech, J. R. (1985). Learning to read: a cognitive
    approach to reading and poor reading. London:
    Croom Helm.
Benbow, C. (1983). Achievement in mathematics (letter).
    Science, 223, 1247.
Bender, L. (1957). Specific reading disability as a
    maturational lag. Bulletin: Orton Society, 7, 9 -
    18.
Bennett, N. (1976). Teaching Styles and Pupil Progress.
    London: Open Books.

Benson, D. F. and Weir, W. F. (1972). Acalculia: acquired anarithmetica. Cortex, 8, 465 - 472.

Bereiter, C. (1980). Development in writing. In Gregg, L. W. and Steinberg, E. R., Cognitive processes in writing. Hillsdale, N.J.: L. Erlbaum, 73 - 93.

Bieger, E. (1974). Effectiveness of visual perceptual training on reading skills of non-readers: An experimental study. Perceptual and Motor Skills, 38, 1147 - 53.

Bieger, E. (1978). Effectiveness of visual training of letters and words on reading skills of non-readers. Journal of Educational Research, 71, 157 - 161.

Birch, H. G. and Belmont, L. (1965). Lateral dominance, lateral awareness and reading disability. Child Development, 36, 57 - 71.

Blank, M. and Solomon, F. (1972). How shall the disadvantaged child be taught? In Cashdan, A. Language in Education. London: Routledge and Kegan Paul.

Blaue, D. and Engelhardt, J. (1984). Maths. clinics: The implications for children in special needs in G.B. Remedial Education, 19, (3), 101 - 107.

Bloodstein, O. N. (1960). The development of stuttering. Journal of Speech and Learning Disorders, 25, 219 - 37.

Bloodstein, O. N. (1960). The development of stuttering. Journal of Speech and Learning Disorders, 25, 366 - 76.

Bloodstein, O. N. (1960). The development of stuttering. Journal of Speech and Learning Disorders, 26, 67 - 82.

Boder, E. (1971). Development dyslexia prevailing diagnostic concepts and a new diagnostic approach. In Myklebust, H. R. (ed.), Progress in Learning Disabilities, 3, 85 - 121. New York: Grune and Stratton.

Boder, E. (1973). Developmental dyslexia: a diagnostic approach based on three atypical reading-spelling patterns. Developmental Medicine and Child Neurology, 15, 663 - 687.

Boller, F. and Graffman, J. (1983). Acalculia: Historical development and current significance. Brain and Cognition, 2, 205 - 223.

Bradley, L. (1981). The organisation of motor patterns for spelling: An effective remedial strategy for backward readers. Developmental Medicine and Child Neurology, 23, 83 - 91.

Bradley, L. (1984). Assessing reading difficulties: A diagnostic and remedial approach. London and Basingstoke: Macmillan.

Bradley, L. and Bryant, P. E. (1978). Difficulties in auditory organisation as a possible cause of reading backwardness. Nature, 271, 746 - 747.

Bradley, L. and Bryant, P. E. (1983). Categorizing sounds and learning to read: A causal connexion. Nature, 301, 419 - 21.

Bradley, L. and Bryant, P. E. (1985). Rhyme and reason in reading and spelling. Ann Arbor: University of Michigan Press.

Brandon, S. and Harris, M. (1967). Stammering: an experimental treatment programme using syllable tuned speech. British Journal of Disorders in Communication, 2, 64 - 8.

Brennan, W. (1982). Changing special education. Milton Keynes: Open University Press.

Brenner, M. W., Gillman, S., Zangwill, O. L. and Farrell, M. (1967). Visuo-motor disability in schoolchildren. British Medical Journal, 4, 259 - 262.

Britton, J., Burgess, T., Martin, N., McLeod, A. and Roch, H. (1975). The development of writing abilities 11-18. London: Macmillan.

Broverman, D., Klarber, R., Kobayashi, E. and Vogel, W. (1968). Rolls of activation and inhibition in sex differences in cognitive abilities. Psychology Review, 75, 23 - 50.

Brown, J.S. and Burton, R.R. (1978). Diagnostic models for procedural bugs in basic mathematical skills. Cognitive Science, 2, 155 - 192.

Brown, N. (1983). A new approach to the treatment of unexpected reading and spelling difficulties. Bulletin of the British Psychological Society, 36, A47 - A48.

Brown, R. and Elliot, R. (1965). The Dynamics of Agression. Journal of Experimental Child Psychology, 12, 103 - 107.

Bruner, J.S. (1964). Some theorems of instruction illustrated with reference to mathematics. The sixty third Yearbook of the National Society for the Study of Education, 1, 63, 306 - 335.

Bruner, J. (1971). The relevance of education. Harmondsworth, Middlesex: Penguin.

Brush, L. (1979). Encouraging girls in mathematics: the problem and solution. Cambridge, Mass.: Abt Associates Press.

Bruskin, C. and Blank, M. (1984). The effects of word class on children's reading and spelling. Brain in Language, 21, 219 - 232.

Bryan, T. (1974). Peer popularity of learning-disabled children. Journal of Learning Disabilities, 7, 624

- 625.

Bryan, T. (1976). Peer popularity of learning-disabled children. A replication. Journal of Learning Difficulties, 307 - 311.

Bryan, T. (1978). Social relationships and verbal interactions of learning disabled children. Journal of Learning Disabilities, 11, 107 - 115.

Bryant, P. and Bradley, L. (1980). Why children sometimes write words which they do not read. In Frith, U., Cognitive Processes in Spelling. London: Academic Press.

Bryant, P. and Bradley, L. (1983). Psychological strategies in the development of reading and writing. In Martlew, M., The psychology of written language. Chichester: John Wiley.

Buffery, A. and Gray, J. (1972). Sex differences in the development of spatial and linguistic skills. In Ounsted, C. and Taylor, D.C. (eds.), Gender differences: Their ontogeny and significance. Baltimore: Williams and Witkins.

Burns, R. B. (1979). The self concept in theory, measurement development and behaviour. London and New York: Longman.

Carpenter, T., Moser, J. and Romberg, T. (1982). Addition and subtraction: A cognitive perspective. Hillsdale, New Jersey: L. Erlbaum.

Cave, C. and Maddison, P. (1978). A survey of recent research in Special Education. Slough: N.F.E.R.

Chall, J. (1967). Learning to read: The great debate. New York: McGraw Hill.

Chandler, M.J. (1973). Egocentrism and anti-social behaviour: The assessment and training of social perspective taking skills. Developmental Psychology, 9, 326 - 332.

Chazan, M. and Laing, A. (1982). The early years. Milton Keynes: Open University Press.

Child, D. (1978). Psychology and the teacher. London: Holt, Rhinehart and Winston.

Choat, E. (1980). Mathematics and the primary school curriculum. Windsor, Berks: N.F.E.R.

Clark, M. M. (1970). Reading difficulties in schools. Harmondsworth: Penguin.

Clark, M. M. (1976). Young fluent readers. London: Heinemann.

Cockcroft, W. H. (1982). Mathematics counts. Report of the Committee of Inquiry into the teaching of mathematics in schools. London: H.M.S.O.

Cohn, R. (1961). Delayed acquisition of reading and writing abilities in children. Archives of Neurology, 4, 153 - 164.

Cohn, R. (1961). Dyscalculia. Archives of Neurology, 4, 301 - 317.

Coltheart, M. (1982). Acquired and developmental dyslexia. Speech and Language Forum, Belfast Whitla Medical Centre. 29 October 1982.

Coltheart, M. (1985). Cognitive neuropsychology and language disorders. Lecture given at short course on cognitive neuropsychology, Birkbeck College: London.

Coltheart, M., Patterson, K. and Marshall, J. (eds.). (1980). Deep dyslexia. London: Routledge and Kegan Paul.

Conrad, R. (1979). The deaf school child. London: Harper and Row.

Critchley, M. (1970). The dyslexic child. London: Heinemann.

Crystal, D. (1980). Introduction to language pathology. London: Arnold.

Crystal, D., Fletcher, P. and Garman, M. (1976). The grammatical analysis of language disability: a procedure for assessment and remediation. London: Arnold.

Cunningham, M. and Murphy, P. (1981). The effects of bilateral EEG biofeedback on verbal, visuo-spatial and creative skills in learning disabled male adolescents. Journal of Learning Disabilities, 14, 204 - 208.

Cutler, A. and McShane, R. (1962). The Trachenberg system of basic maths. London: Souvenir Press.

Dalton, P. and Hardcastle, W.J. (1977). Disorders of fluency. London: Arnold.

Daniels, J. C. and Diack, H. (1958). The standard reading tests. London: Chatto and Windus.

Dawdy, S. C. (1981). Paediatric neuropsychology: Caring for the developmentally dyspraxic child. Clinical Neuropsychology, 3, 30 - 37.

Dean, P. (1982). Teaching and learning mathematics. London: Woburn Press.

DeHirsch, K, Jansky, J. J. and Langford, W. S. (1966). Predicting reading failure: A preliminary study. New York: Harper and Row.

Denvir, B., Stolz, C. and Brown, M. (1982). Low attainers in mathematics 5-16. Schools Council Working Paper 72. London: Methuen Educational.

D.E.S. (1972). Children with specific reading difficulties. Tizard Report. London: H.M.S.O.

D.E.S. (1978). Primary education in England. Survey by H.M.I. London: H.M.S.O.

D.E.S. (1979). Aspects of Secondary Education in England. Survey by H.M.I. London: H.M.S.O.

Dienes, Z. P. and Jeeves, M. A. (1969). Thinking in Structures. London: Hutchinson.

Doehring, D. G. (1968). Patterns of impairment in specific reading disability. Indiana University Press.

Donachy, W. (1975). Renfrewshire pre-school project. Scottish Education Department magazine.

Donachy, W. (1976). Parent participation in pre-school education. British Journal of Educational Psychology, 46, 31 - 3.

Donaldson, M. (1978). Children's minds. Glasgow: Fontana/Collins.

Downing, J. and Leong, C. (1983). The psychology of reading. London: Holt, Rinehardt and Winston.

Downing, J. and Thackray, D. V. (1971). Reading readiness. U.K.R.A. Univ. London Press.

Early, G., Nelson, D. A., Kleber, D. J., Treegoob, M., Huffman, E. and Cass, C. (1976). Cursive handwriting, reading and spelling achievement. Academic Therapy, 12, 67 - 74.

Egger, J., Carter, C. M., Graham, P. J., Gumley, D. and Soothill, J. F. (1985). Controlled trial of oligoantigenic treatment in the hyperkinetic syndrome. The Lancet, 540 - 545.

Ellis, A. W. (1982). Spelling and writing (and reading and speaking). Normality and pathology in cognitive functions, 4. London: Academic Press.

Ellis, A. W. (1984). Reading, writing and dyslexia: a cognitive analysis. London: L. Erlbaum

Fairman, I. F. (1972). Tackling the cumulative reading handicap. London Education Review 1.

Farnham-Diggory, S. (1978). Learning disabilities. London: Fontana/Open Books.

Feingold, B. F. (1975). Why your child is hyperactive. New York: Random House.

Fennema, E. (1974). Mathematics learning and the sexes: a review. Journal of Research in Mathematics Education, 5, 129 - 139.

Fennema, E. (1979). Women and girls in mathematics. Educational studies in Mathematics, 10, 389 - 401.

Fernald, G. M. (1921). The effect of kinaesthesic factors in the development of word recognition in the case of the poor reader. Journal of Educational Research, 4, 355 - 77.

Fernald, G. M. (1943). Remedial techniques in basic school subjects. New York: McGraw Hill.

Fogelman, K. (1976). Britain's 16-year-olds. London: National Children's Bureau.

Foster, K. and Torgesen, J. (1983). The effects of directed study on the spelling performance of two subgroups of learning disabled students. <u>Learning Disability Quarterly</u>, 252 - 257.

Foxman, D., Gresswell, M., Ward, M., Badger, M., Tusan, J. and Bloomfeld, B. (1978). Mathematical development. <u>Primary Survey Report No. 1.</u> Assessment of Performance Unit, D.E.S. London: H.M.S.O.

Foxman, D. D., Ruddock, G. J., Badger, M. E. and Martini, R. M. (1980). Mathematical Development. <u>Primary Survey Report No. 3.</u> Assessment of Performance Unit, D.E.S. London: H.M.S.O.

Fransella, F. (1972). <u>Personal change and reconstruction.</u> London: Academic Press.

Frary, R. B. and Ling, J. (1983). A factor analytic study of mathematics anxiety. <u>Educational and Psychological Measurement</u>, 43, 985 - 994.

Frith, U. (1980). <u>Cognitive processes in spelling.</u> London: Academic Press.

Froebel, F. (1912). <u>Pedagogics of the kindergarten or ideas concerning the play of children.</u> Engelwood Cliffs, N.J.: Appleton.

Frostig, M. (1976). <u>Education for dignity.</u> New York: Grune and Stratton.

Frostig, M. and Horne, D. (1973). The Frostig Program for the development of visual perception. Developmental Education. Chicago: Follet.

Frostig, M. and Maslow, P. (1973). <u>Learning problems in the classroom: Prevention and remediation.</u> New York: Grune and Stratton.

Frostig, M., Lefener, W. and Whittlesey, M. S. (1966). Developmental test of visual perception. <u>Administration and scoring manual.</u> Palo Alto, California: Consulting Psychologists Press.

Fry, C. L. (1969). Training children to communicate to listeners who have varying listening requirements. Journal of Genetic Psychology, 114, 153 - 166.

Fry, M. A., Johnson, C. S. and Muehl, S. (1970). Oral language production in relation to reading achievement among select second graders. In Bakker, D. and Satz, P., <u>Specific reading disability.</u> Rotterdam University Press.

Fundudis, T., Kolvin, I. and Garside, R. F. (1979). <u>Speech retarded and deaf children: their psychological development.</u> New York: Academic Press.

Furth, H. G. (1971). Linguistic deficiency and thinking: research with deaf subjects, 1964 - 69. <u>Psychological Bulletin</u>, 76, 58 - 72.

Furth, H. and Youniss, J. (1975). Convenital deafness

and the development of thinking. In Lenneberg, E. H. and Lenneberg, E. (eds.), Foundation of language development: A multidisciplinary approach. New York: Academic Press.

Gagné, R. M. (1970). The conditions of learning. New York: Holt, Rhinehart and Winston.

Gagné, R. M. and Briggs, L. J. (1974). Principles of instructional design. New York: Holt, Rhinehart and Winston.

Ganschow, L. (1984). Analysis of error patterns to remediate severe spelling difficulties. The Reading Teacher, 38, 3, 288 - 293.

Garman, M. (1980). Using LARSP in assessment and remediation. In Jones, F. M., Language disability in children. Lancaster: M.T.P. Press.

Geschwind, N. (1964). The development of the brain and the evolution of language. Monograph Series on Language and Linguistics, 17, 155 - 169.

Gettinger, M., Bryant, N. D. and Fayne, H. (1982). Designing spelling instructions for learning disabled children: An emphasis on unit size, distributed practice and training for transfer. Journal of Special Education, 16, 439 - 448.

Gibson, E. (1965). Learning to read. In Science, 148, 1066 - 1072. Also in Singer, H. and Ruddell, R. (1976). Theoretical models and processes in reading, Newark, Del.: International Reading Association.

Gibson, E. and Levin, H. (1975). The psychology of reading. Cambridge: M.I.T. Press.

Gillingham, A. and Stillman, B. (1956). Remedial training for children with specific disabilities in reading, writing and penmanship, 5th edn. Cambridge, Mass.: Education Publishing Services Ltd.

Ginsburg, H. (1977). Children's arithmetic: The learning process. New York: Van Nostrand.

Giordano, G. (1983). The pivotal role of grammar in correcting writing disabilities. Journal of Special Education, 17, 473 - 481.

Glaser, R. (1978). Advances in Instructional Psychology, 1. Hillsdale, N.J.: L. Erlbaum.

Golden, G. (1984). Controversial therapies. In Shaywitz, S., Grossman, H. Z. and Shaywitz, B., Symposium on learning disorders. The Paediatric Clinic of North America, 31. London: Sanders.

Goodenough, F.L. (1926). Measurement of intelligence by drawings. New York: World Books.

Goodman, K. S. (1969). Analysis of oral reading miscues: applied psycholinguistics. Reading

Research Quarterly, 5, (1), 9 - 30.

Goodman, K. S. (ed.) (1973). Miscue Analysis: Application to reading instruction. Urbana, Illinois: ERIC Clearinghouse on reading and comprehension skills. National Council for Teachers of English.

Gordon, N. and Grimley, A. (1974). Clumsiness and perceptual-motor disorders in children. Physiotherapy, 60, 311 - 315.

Gordon, N. and McKinlay, I. (eds.) (1980). Helping clumsy children. Edinburgh: Churchill Livingstone.

Gottman, J. M. (1983). How children become friends. Monograph of the Society for Research in Child Development. Vol.48, No.3, Serial No.201.

Great Britain. (1980). Special needs in Education. Cmd. paper, 7996. London: HMSO.

Great Britain. (1981). Education Act. Public and General Acts, Part II, 1507. London: HMSO.

Gredler, G. (1972). Severe reading disability: some important correlates. In Reid, J., Reading: Problems and Practices. London: Ward Lock Educational.

Greenberg, L. and Lipman, R. (1971). Pharmacotherapy of hyperactive children. Clinical proceedings of the Children's Hospital, Washington, 27, 101.

Gregg, L. W. and Steinberg, E. R. (1980). Cognitive processes in writing. Hillsdale, N.J.: L. Erlbaum.

Grumlach, R. (1981). On the nature and development of children's writing. In Fredericksen, C. and Dominic, J. F., Writing: the nature, development and teaching of written communication. Hillsdale, N.J.: L. Erlbaum.

Grunwell, P. (1980). Developmental language disorders at the phonological level. In Jones, F. B., Language disability in children. Lancaster: MTP Press.

Gubbay, S. S. (1975). The clumsy child. London: Saunders.

Gubbay, S. S., Ellis, E., Walton, J. N. and Court, S. D. M. (1965). Clumsy children: A study of apraxic and agnosic defects in 21 children. Brain, 88, 295 - 312.

Guilford, J. P. (1959). Three faces of intellect. American Psychologist, 14.

Harding, L. M. (1983). The relationship between reading ability and developmental levels in primary school children. Unpublished D.Phil. thesis. New University of Ulster.

Harding, L. M. (1984). Reading errors and style in children with a specific reading disability.

Journal of Research in Reading, 7, 103 - 112.

Harding, L. M. and McLaughan, S. (1985). Integration for Better? Paper presented at the International Conference on Special Education, Nottingham University. July 1985.

Harding, L. M., Beech, J. R. and Sneddon, W. (1985). The changing pattern of reading errors and reading style from 5 to 11 years of age. British Journal of Educational Psychology, 55, 45 - 52.

Harley, J. P., Ray, R. S. and Tomasi, L. (1978). Hyperkinesis and food additives: Testing the Feingold hypothesis. Paediatrics, 61, 818 - 28.

Harris, D. B. (1963). Children's drawings as measure of intellectual maturity. New York: Harcourt Brace.

Harrop, A. and McCann, C. (1984). Modifying 'creative writing' in the classroom. British Journal of Education Psychology, 54, 62 - 72.

Hart, K. M. (ed.) (1981). Children's understanding of mathematics 11-16. London: John Murray.

Hecaen, H. (1962). Clinical symptomatology in right and left hemispheric lesions. In Mountcastle, J., Interhemispheric relations and cerebral dominance. Baltimore: John Hopkins.

Hegarty, S., Pocklington, R. and Lucas, D. (1981). Educating pupils with special needs in the ordinary school. Windsor: NFER.

Henderson, S. E. and Hall, D. (1982). Concomitants of clumsiness in young school children. Developmental Medicine and Child Neurology, 24, 448 - 460.

Herbert, M. (1975). Emotional problem of development in children. London: Pan.

Herbert, M. (1981). Behavioural treatment of problem children: a practise manual. London: Academic Press.

Hermann, K. and Norrie, E. (1958). Is congenital word blindness a hereditary type of Gerstmann's syndrome? Psychiatria and Neurologia, 136, 59 - 73.

Hewett, J. (1967). Educating emotionally disturbed children. Exceptional children, 33, 459 - 467.

Hewett, J. (1969). The engineered classroom. In Dupont, B., Educating emotionally disturbed children. New York: Harcourt Brace.

Hicks, C. and Spurgeon, P. (1982). Two factor analytic studies of dyslexic subtypes. British Journal of Educational Psychology, 52, 289 - 300.

Hinshelwood, J. (1917). Congenital word blindness. London: Lewis.

Holt, J. (1966). How children fail. Harmondsworth: Penguin.

Holt, K. S. (1975). Movement and child development clinics in developmental medicine. Spastics International Publishing Ltd. London: Heinemann.

Homan, D. (1970). The child with learning disabilities in arithmetic. Arithmetic teacher, 19, 131 - 133.

Hornsby, B. and Miles, T. (1980). The effects of a dyslexia-centred teaching programme. British Journal of Educational Psychology, 50, 236 - 42.

Hornsby, B. and Shear, F. (1980). Alpha to Omega. Wisbech, Cambridgeshire: Learning Development Aids.

Hughes, M. (1955). Relationship of maturation to writing. In Carr, C. (ed.), When children write, 7 - 15. Washington: Association for Childhood Education.

Hulme, C. (1981). Reading retardation and multisensory teaching. London: Routledge and Kegan Paul.

Hulme, C. and Bradley, L. (1984). An experimental study of multi-sensory teaching with normal and retarded readers. In Malatesha, R. N. and Whitaker, H. A. (eds.), Dyslexia: a global issue. The Hague: Martinus Nihoff.

Hulme, C., Smart, A. and Moran, G. (1982). Visual perceptual deficits in clumsy children. Neuropsychologia, 20, 475 - 481.

Hulme, C., Biggerstaff, A., Moran, G. and McKinlay, I. (1982). Visual, kinaesthetic and cross-modal judgements of length by normal and clumsy children. Developmental Medicine and Child Neurology, 24, 461 - 471.

Humphreys, G. (1985). Neurological disorders of visual perception. Lecture given at short course on cognitive neuropsychology. Birkbeck College, London.

Hunt, J. Mc.V. (1961). Intelligence and experience. New York: Ronald Press.

Ingram, D. (1976). Phonological disability in children. London: Arnold.

Irwin, A. (1972). The treatment and results of easy stammering. British Journal of Disorders in Communication, 7, 151 - 6.

Joffe, L. S. (1980). Dyslexia and attainment in school maths. Dyslexia Review, Winter, 12 - 18.

Joffe, L. S. (1983). Book Review. Low attainment in mathematics 5-16. Schools Council WP 72. Educational Research, 25, 147 - 148.

Johnson, D. J. and Myklebust, H. R. (1967). Learning disabilities. New York: Grune and Stratton.

Johnson, W. (1939). The treatment of stuttering. Journal of Speech Disorders, 4, 170 - 2.

Jones, D. (1983). Computer-based remedial spelling

instructions. *Bulletin of the British Psychological Society*, 36, A60 - A61.

Jorm, A. F. (1979). The cognitive and neurological basis of developmental dyslexia: a theoretical framework and review. *Cognition*, 7, 19 - 33.

Kephart, N. C. (1970). *The slow learner in the classroom*. 2nd ed. Columbus, Ohio: Merrill.

Kinsbourne, M. and Warrington, E. (1963). The Developmental Gerstmann Syndrome. *Archives of Neurology*, 8, 490 - 501.

Kinsbourne, M. and Warrington, E. (1966). Developmental factors in reading and writing backwardness. In Money, J. and Schiffman, G., *The disabled reader*. Baltimore: John Hopkins Press.

Kirk, S. and Kirk, W. (1966). *The diagnostic and remediation of psycholinguistic disabilities*. University of Illinois Press.

Kirk, S. A., McCarthy, J. J. and Kirk, W. D. (1968). Examiners' manual. *Illinois test of psycholinguistic abilities*. Board of Trustees, University of Illinois. Available from NFER, Staines, Middlesex.

Kohl, H. (1970). *The open classroom: A practical guide to a way of teaching*. London: Methuen.

Koppitz, E. M. (1963). *The Bender Gestalt Test for young children*. New York: Grune and Stratton.

Kosc, L. (1974). Developmental dyscalculia. *Journal of Learning Disabilities*, 7, 164 - 177.

Krutetskii, V. A. (1976). *The psychology of mathematical abilities in schoolchildren*. Transl. by J. Teller. Chicago and London: University of Chicago Press.

Landsdown, R. (1978). Retardation in mathematics: a consideration of multifactorial determination. *Journal of Child Psychology and Psychiatry*, 19, 181 - 185.

Lapouse, R. and Monk, M. A. (1958). An epidemiological study of behaviour characteristics in children. *American Journal of Public Health*, 48, 1134.

Lehr, F. (1984). Spelling instruction, phonics rules and word lists. *The Reading Teacher*, 38, 2, 218 - 220.

Lenneberg, E. H. (1967). *Biological foundations of language*. New York: Wiley.

Leong, Che K. (1976). Lateralization in severely disabled readers in relation to functional cerebral development and synthesis of information. In Knights, D. and Bakker, P. *The neuropsychology of learning disorders*. Baltimore, London, Tokyo: University Park Press.

Lerner, J. (1971). Learning disabilities: Their diagnosis and teaching strategies. (3rd edn.) Boston, Ma.: Houghton Mifflin.

Levy, A. (1976). Understanding a process. ILEA Contact, 5, 14.

Lindsay, G. A. and McLennan, D. (1984). Lined paper: its effects on the legibility and creativity of young children's writing. British Journal of Educational Psychology, 53, 364 - 368.

Loban, W. D. (1976). Language development: kindergarten through grade 12. Research Report No. 18. Urbana, Illinois: NCTE.

Lovell, K. and Gorton, A. (1968). A study of some differences between backward and normal readers of average intelligence. British Journal of Educational Psychology, 87, 240 - 247.

Lorigho, L. (1981). Mathematics and the brain: a tale of two hemispheres. The Massachusetts teacher, 60 (5), 8 - 12.

Luria, A. R. (1966). Human brain and psychological processes. New York and London: Harper and Row.

Luria, A. R. (1973). The working brain. Harmondsworth: Penguin.

Lyle, J. G. (1969). Reading retardation and reversal tendency: A factorial study. Child Development, 40, 833 - 843.

McCarthy, J. and Kirk, S. (1961). Illinois test of psycholinguistic abilities. Institute for research on exceptional children, University of Illinois.

McCleod, T. M. and Clump, W. D. (1978). The relationship of visuo-spatial and verbal ability to learning disabilities in mathematics. Journal of Learning Disabilities, 11, 237 - 241.

McCreesh, J. and Maher, A. (1974). Remedial Education: objectives and techniques. London: Ward Lock Educational.

McKinley, I. (1978). Strategies for clumsy children. Developmental Medicine and Child Neurology, 20, 495 - 501.

McLeod, J. and Atkinson, J. (1972). Domain Phonic Test Manual. Edinburgh: Oliver and Boyd.

Madden, R., Gardner, E., Rudman, H., Karlsen, B. and Merwin, J. (1973). The Stanford Achievement Test. New York: Harcourt Brace Janovich.

Magné, O. (1978). The psychology of remedial mathematics. Didakometry (Malmo School of Education, Sweden), 10, 59.

Marcie, P. (1983). Writing disorders associated with

focal cortical lesions. In Martlew, M., The psychology of written language. Chichester: Wiley.

Martlew, M. (1983). Problems and difficulties: Cognitive and communicative aspects of writing. In Martlew, M., The psychology of written language. Chichester: Wiley.

Mattis, S. (1981). Dyslexia syndromes in children. In Pirozzolo, F. and Wiltrock, C., Neuropsychological and cognitive processes in reading, New York: Academic Press.

Mattis, S., French, J. H. and Rapin, I. (1975). Dyslexia in children and young adults: three independent neuropsychological syndromes. Developmental Medicine and Child Neurology, 17, 150 - 163.

Meichenbaum, D. (1975). Self instruction methods. In Kaifer, F. and Goldstein, A. (eds.), Helping people change. New York: Pergamon Press.

Merrit, J. (1972). Reading failure: a re-examination. In Southgate, V. (ed.), Literacy at all levels, London: Ward Lock Educational.

Miles, T. R. (1970). On helping the dyslexic child. London: Methuen.

Miles, T. R. (1983). Dyslexia: the pattern of difficulties. St. Albans, Herts.: Granada.

Miller, K. and Gelman, R. (1983). The child's representation of numbers: a multidimensional scaling analysis. Child Development, 54, 1470 - 1479.

Milton, G. A. (1959). Sex differences in problem solving as a function of the role appropriateness of the problem content. Psychological Report, 5, 705 - 8.

Minskoff, E. (1980). Teaching approach for developing non-verbal communication skills in students with social perception deficits. Journal of Learning Disabilities, 13, 118 - 124.

Monroe, M. (1932). Children who cannot read. University of Chicago Press.

Montessori, M. (1945). The Montessori Method. London: Heinemann.

Morley, M. E. (1957). The development and disorders of speech in childhood. Livingstone: Churchill.

Morris, J. M. (1966). Standards of progress in reading. Slough: NFER.

Muller, D., Munro, S. and Code, C. (1981). Language assessment for remediation. London: Croom Helm.

Myklebust, H. R. (1964). The psychiatry of deafness. New York: Grune and Stratton.

Myklebust, H. R. (1967). Development and disorders of

written language. The Picture Story Language Test, Vol.1. New York: Grune and Stratton.

Myklebust, H. R. (1975). Non-verbal learning disabilities: Assessment and interventions. In Myklebust, H., Progress in Learning Disabilities, 3, 85 - 121. New York: Grune and Stratton.

Myklebust, H. R. (1980). What is the future for learning disability? Journal of Learning Disabilities, 13, 468 - 471.

Naidoo, S. (1972). Specific Dyslexia: The research report of the ICCA Word Blindness Centre for dyslexic children. London: Pitman.

Naidoo, S. (1981). Teaching methods and their rationale. In Pavladis, G. T. and Miles, T. R. (eds.), Dyslexia research and its application to education. London: J. Wiley.

Nash, S. (1978). Sex role as a mediator of intellectual functioning. In Wittig, M. A. and Petersen, A. C. (eds.), Sex related differences in cognitive functioning: developmental issues. New York: Academic Press.

Nelson, H. and Warrington, K. (1974). Developmental spelling retardation and its relation to other cognitive abilities. British Journal of Psychology, 65, 265 - 274.

Neuman, S. B. (1981). Effect of teaching auditory perceptual skills in reading achievement in first grade. Reading Teacher, 34, 422 - 426.

Newell, P. (1983). ACE Special Education Handbook: The new law on children with Special Education needs. London: Advisory Centre for Education.

Olson, O. (1977). Oral and written language and the cognitive processes of children. Journal of Communication, 27, 3, 10 - 26.

Orton, S. (1937). Reading, writing and speech problems in children. New York: Norton.

Osborn, H. (1983). The assessment of mathematical abilities. Educational Research, 25, 28 - 40.

Owen, F. W., Adams, P. A., Forrest, T., Stolz, L. and Fisher, S. (1971). Learning disorders in children: Sibling studies. Monograph of the society for research in child development, 144, 36, 4.

Patterson, K. E., Marshall, J. C. and Coltheart, M. (1985). Surface dyslexia: Neuropsychological and cognitive studies of phonological reading. London: L. Erlbaum.

Patterson, K. and Shewell, K. (1986). In Humphreys, G., Short course in cognitive neuropsychology. Birkbeck College, London.

171

Pavladis, G. T. (1982). What makes dyslexics distinctly different from backward readers? Bulletin of the British Psychological Society, 35, 118.

Peters, M. (1967). Spelling: caught or taught. London: Routledge and Kegan Paul.

Peters, M. (1970). Success in spelling. Cambridge: Hefler.

Petrauskas, R. and Rourke, B. (1979). Identification of subtypes of retarded readers: A neuropsychological, multivariate approach. Journal of Clinical Neuropsychology, 1, 17 - 37.

Piaget, J. (1953). The child's concept of number. London: Routledge and Kegan Paul.

Piaget, J. (1956). Language and thought from the genetic point of view. In Elkind, D. (ed.), (1967), Psychological studies. Random House. And in Adams, P. (1972). Language in Thinking. Harmondsworth: Penguin.

Piaget, J. (1964). Quotations. In Ripple, R. E. and Rockcastle, V. N., (eds.) Piaget rediscovered. Ithaca, New York: Carnell University Press.

Piaget, J. and Inhelder, B. (1969). The psychology of the child. London: Routledge and Kegan Paul.

Pidgeon, D. (1967). Achievement in mathematics. Slough, Bucks.: NFER.

Plowden, Lady Bridget H. (1967). Children and their primary schools. A report of the Central Advisory Council for Education (England), Vols. 1 and 2. London: HMSO.

Pringle, K. M., Butler, N. R. and Davie, R. (1966). 11,000 Seven-year-olds: Studies in Child Development. London: Longmans.

Purden-Smith, J. and De Severe, D. (1982). The Maths Gene. Readers Digest, Nov. 263.

Quirk Report. (1972). Speech therapy services. London: HMSO.

Rae, G. and McPhillimy, W. N. (1971). Learning in the primary school. London: Hodder and Stoughton.

Raskin, L. (1984). Neurochemical correlates of attention deficit syndrome. In Shaywitz, S, Grossman, H. Z. and Shaywitz, B., Symposium on learning disorders. The Paediatric Church of North America, 31. London: Sanders.

Read, C. (1971). Preschool children's knowledge of English phonology. Harvard Educational Review, 41, 1 - 34.

Read, C. (1981). Writing is not the inverse of reading in young children. In Fredericksen, C. and Dominic, J. F., Writing: the nature development and teaching of written communication. Hillsdale,

N.J.: L. Erlbaum.

Rees, R. (1983). The structure of mathematical ability: A further study. Bulletin of the British Psychological Society, 36, A66.

Reid, J. F. (1972). Dyslexia: a problem of communication. In Reid, J. F. Reading problems and practises. London: Ward Lock.

Renfrew, C.E. (1966). Speech disorders in children. Oxford: Pergamon International Library.

Resnick, L. B. and Ford, W. W. (1981). The psychology of mathematics for instruction. Hillsdale, N.J.: L. Erlbaum.

Reynell, J. (1969). Test manual: Reynell Developmental Language Scales. Slough: NFER.

Riding, R. J. and Boardman, D. J. (1983). The relationship between sex and learning style and graphicacy in 14-year-old children. Educational Review, 35, 1.

Ross, A. D. (1977). Learning disability: The unrealised potential. New York: McGraw Hill.

Ross, D. M. and Ross, S. A. (1976). Hyperactivity research: Theory and action. Chichester: J. Wiley.

Rourke, B. (1978). Reading, spelling, arithmetic disabilities: A neuropsychologic perspective. In Myklebust, H., Progress in Learning Disabilities, 4, 97 - 121. New York: Grune and Stratton.

Rourke, B. P. and Finlayson, M. A. J. (1978). Neurophysiological significance of variables in posture of academic performance in verbal and visuo-spatial abilities. Journal of Abnormal and Child Psychology, 6, 121 - 131.

Rourke, B. and Strang, J. (1978). Neuropsychological significance of variables in pattern of academic performance: Motor, psychomotor and tactile-perceptual abilities. Journal of Paediatric Psychology, 3, 62 - 66.

Rutter, M., Tizard, J. and Whitmore, K. (1970). Education, health and behaviour. London: Longman.

Ryan, B. P. and Van Kirk, B. (1974). The establishment, transfer and maintenance of fluent speech in 50 stutterers using delayed auditory feedback and operant procedures. Journal of Speech and Hearing Disorders, 39, 3 - 10.

Rye, J. (1982). Cloze procedure and the teaching of reading. London: Heinemann.

Satz, P. and Sparrow, S. (1970). Specific developmental dyslexia: a theoretical formulation. In Baker, D. and Satz, P., Specific reading disability, University of Rotterdam Press.

Satz, P., Taylor, H. G., Friel, J. and Fletcher, J. M.

(1978). Some developmental and predictive
precursors of reading disabilities: a six year
follow-up. In Benton, A. L. and Pearl, D.,
Dyslexia: An appraisal of current knowledge. New
York: Oxford University Press.

Saxe, G. B. and Shaheen, S. (1981). Piagetian theory
and the atypical case: An analysis of the
Developmental Gerstmann Syndrome. Journal of
Learning Disabilities, 14, 131 - 135 and 172.

Sayer, M., Kuchemann, D. E. and Wylam, H. (1976). The
distribution of Piagetian stages of thinking in
British middle and secondary schoolchildren.
British Journal of Educational Psychology, 46, 164
- 173.

Scardamelia, M. (1981). How children cope with the
cognitive demands of writing. In Frederiksen, C.
and Dominic, J. F., Writing: The nature,
development and teaching of written communication.
Hillsdale, N.J.: L. Erlbaum.

Schaffer, D. (1973). Psychiatric aspects of brain
injury in childhood: a review. Developmental
Medicine and Child Neurology, 15, 211 - 220.

Schonell, F. J. (1937). Diagnosis of individual
differences in arithmetic. Edinburgh and London:
Oliver and Boyd.

Schonell, F. J. and Schonell, E. E. (1950). Diagnostic
and attainment testing. Edinburgh and London:
Oliver and Boyd.

Shaffer, D., McNamara, N. and Pincus, J. (1974).
Controlled observations on patterns of activity,
attention and impulsivity in brain damaged and
psychiatrically disturbed boys. Psychological
Medicine, 4, 4.

Shantz, C. V. (1975). The development of social
cognition. Chicago: University of Chicago Press.

Shantz, C. V. and Wilson, K. (1972). Training
communication skills in young children. Child
Development, 43, 118 - 122.

Shaywitz, S. and Shaywitz, B. (1984). Diagnosis and
management of attention deficit disorders. In
Shaywitz, S., Grossman, H. and Shaywitz, M. D.,
Paediatric Clinics of North America, 31, 429 - 459.
London: Saunders.

Shaywitz, S., Grossman, H. Z. and Shaywitz, B. (1984).
Symposium on learning disorders. The Paediatric
Clinics of North America, 31. London: Saunders.

Sheridan, M. D. (1945). The child's acquisition of
speech. British Medical Journal, I, 707.

Shrag, P. and Divoky, D. (1981). The myth of the
hyperactive child. Harmondsworth: Penguin.

Shuard, H. and Quadling, O. (1980). Teachers of mathematics. New York: Harper and Row.

Shuy, R. (1982). Toward a developmental theory of writing. In Fredericksen, C. and Dominic, J. F., Writing: The nature, development and teaching of written communication. Hillsdale, N.J.: L. Erlbaum.

Silver, A. and Hagin, R. (1966). Maturation of perceptual functions in children with specific reading disabilities. The Reading Teacher, 4, 253 - 259.

Skemp, R. (1971). The psychology of learning mathematics. Harmondsworth: Pelican.

Slade, P. D. and Russell, G. F. M. (1971). Developmental dyscalculia: a brief report on four cases. Psychological Medicine, 1, 292 - 298.

Smith, F. (1978). Understanding reading: a psycholinguistic analysis of reading and learning to read, 2nd edn. London: Holt, Rhinehart and Winston.

Smith, F. and Goodman, K. (1971). On the psycholinguistic method of teaching reading. Elementary School Journal, 1.

Smith, M. and Bean, T. (1983). Four strategies that develop children's strong comprehension and writing. The Reading Teacher, 37, 295 - 304.

Snyder, S. D. and Michael, W. B. (1983). The relationship of performance on standardised tests in maths and reading, two measures of social intelligence and one of academic self esteem from two samples of primary school children. Education and Psychological Measurement, 43, 1141 - 1148.

Spearman, C. (1927). The abilities of man. London: Macmillan.

Special Education Forward Trends (1982). Special Education in Parliament, 9, 33.

Spellacy, F. and Peters, B. (1978). Dyscalculia and elements of the Developmental Gerstmann Syndrome. Cortex, 14, 197 - 206.

Stahl, A. (1977). The structure of children's compositions: Development and ethnic differences. Research in the Teaching of English, 11, 156 - 163.

Start, K. B. and Wells, B. K. (1972). The trend of reading standards. Slough: NFER.

Statistics of Education (1977). Vol.1. Schools: England and Wales. London: HMSO.

Statistics of Education (1979). Vol.1. Schools: England and Wales. London: HMSO.

Staub, E. (1971). The use of role playing and induction

in children's learning of helping and sharing behaviour. Child Development, 42, 805 - 816.

Stewart, M. A., Pitts, F. N., Craig, A. G. and Pierfu, W. (1966). The hyperactive child syndrome. American Journal of Orthopsychiatry, 35, 861.

Stott, D. H. (1966). Programmed reading kit. London: Holmes McDougall.

Stott, D. H., Moyes, F. A. and Henderson, G. (1972). Test of motor impairment. University of Guelph, Ontario: Brook International Publishing Corporation.

Strauss, A. and Lehtinen, L. (1947). Psychopathology and education of the brain-injured child. New York: Grune and Stratton.

Strickland, R. G. (1962). The language of elementary school children. Its relationship to the language of reading textbooks and the quality of reading of selected reading. Bulletin 38(4). Indiana University, Bloomington School of Education.

Tansley, P. and Pankhurst, J. (1981). Children with specific learning difficulties: A critical review of research. Windsor, Bucks.: NFER-Nelson.

Thomasson, A. and Tewlings, H. L. (1983). The development of handwriting. In Martlew, M., The psychology of written language. Chichester: J. Wiley.

Thorndike, E. L. (1922). The psychology of arithmetic. New York: Macmillan.

Thurstone, E. L. (1938). Primary mental abilities. Chicago and London: University of Chicago Press.

Tizard, B. and Hughes, M. (1984). Young children learning. London: Fontana.

Tizard, J., Schofield, W. N. and Hewison, J. (1982). Collaboration between teachers and parents in assisting children's reading. British Journal of Educational Psychology, 52, 1 - 15.

Torgesen, J. K. (1977). The role of non-specific factors in the task performance of learning-disabled children: A theoretical assessment. Journal of Learning Disabilities, 10, 27 - 34.

Tough, J. (1976). Listening to children talking: A guide to the appraisal of children's use of language. London: Ward Lock.

Tough, J. (1977). Talking and learning. London: Ward Lock Educational and Drake Educational Associates.

Van Riper, C. (1971). The nature of stuttering. Englewood Cliffs, N.J.: Prentice Hall.

Van Riper, C. (1973). The treatment of stuttering. Englewood Cliffs, N.J.: Prentice Hall.

Vellutino, F. (1980). Dyslexia: perceptual deficiency or perceptual inefficiency. In Kavanagh, J. F. and Venezky, R. L., Orthography, reading and dyslexia. Baltimore: University Park Press.

Vernon, M. D. (1979). Variability in reading retardation. British Journal of Psychology, 70, 7 - 16.

Vernon, P. E. (1961). The structure of human abilities, 2nd edn. London: McMillan.

Walton, J. N., Ellis, E. and Court, S. D. M. (1962). Clumsy children: Developmental apraxia and agnosia. Brain, 85, 603 - 612.

Ward, M. (1979). Mathematics and the 10-year-old. Schools Council Working Paper 61. London: Evans/Methuen Educational.

Warnock, H. M. (1978). Report of the committee of inquiry into the education of handicapped children and young people. London: HMSO.

Watson, P. (1981). Personality and arithmetic of normal school pupils and boys in a community home with education. British Journal of Educational Psychology, 51, 394 - 397.

Weber, K. (1978). Yes, they can. New York: International Publishing Service.

Wedell, K. (1972). Learning and perceptive-motor disabilities in children. London: Wiley.

Wedell, K. (1975). Orientation in special education. Chichester: J. Wiley.

Wedell, K., Welton, J. and Vorhaus, G. (1982). Challenges in the 1981 Act. Special Education Forward Trends, 9, 6 - 8.

Weinstein, M. (1980). A neuropsychological approach to maths disability. New York University Education Quarterly, 11, 22 - 28.

Weiss, D. A. (1964). Cluttering. Englewood Cliffs, New Jersey: Prentice Hall.

Wepman, J. (1958). Auditory discrimination test. III. Chicago: Language Research Association.

Werdelin, I. (1958). The mathematical ability. Copenhagen: Lund.

Whalen, C. K. and Henker, B. (eds.) (1980). Hyperactive children: the social ecology of identification and treatment. New York: Academic Press.

Whaley, D. L. and Malott, R. W. (1971). Elementary principles of behaviour. New York: Appleton Century Crofts.

Wheeler, L. J. and McNutt, G. (1982). The effect of syntax on low achieving students' abilities to solve mathematical hard problems. Journal of Special Education, 17, 309 - 315.

Wiig, E. H. and Harris, S. P. (1974). Perception and interpretation of non-verbally expressed emotions by adolescents with learning disabilities. Perceptual and Motor Skills, 38, 239 - 245.

Witelson, S. (1976). Sex and the single hemisphere. Science, 425 - 427.

Witelson, S. (1977). Developmental dyslexia: Two right hemispheres and none left. Science, 195, 309 - 11.

Wolfendale, S. and Bryans, T. (1978). Identification of learning difficulties. A model for intervention. National Association for Remedial Education.

Wong, B. and Wong, R. (1980). Role-taking skills in normal achieving and learning-disabled children. Learning Disability Quarterly, 3, 11 - 18.

Woods, C.L. (1984). Social position and speaking competence in stuttering and normally fluent boys. Journal of Speech and Hearing Research, 17, 740 - 7.

Zigler, E. (1968). Rigidity in the retarded. In Trapp, H. and Himmelstein, M., Readings on the exceptional child. New York: Academic Press.

counselling
  stuttering and 39
creative 11
curriculum 3, 92

deaf 6, 20, 23
  communication in 24
  language output 24
  manual sign language 24
  reading 25
  thinking 25
decoding 15, 17
deficit 13
delicate 6
developmental dysgraphia 81
developmental dyslexia 50
  subgroups 50
developmental language
  disorders 22-3, 27-33, 78
  auditory discrimination
    and 27
  check list for 28
  grammar 30
  remediation 31
diagnostic hypotheses 2
diagnostic-remedial method
  3, 15
diet
  hyperactivity and 106-7
disinhibition 17
Down's syndrome 13, 34
drugs
  hyperactivity and 105
dysarthria 22, 27
  154-6
dyscalculia 121, 124-5
dysfluency 36, 37
dyslexia 44
  adults 49
  auditory-verbal 58, 85
  developmental 50
  intelligence and 44
  subgroups 50
  visual-motor problems
    53, 85
dyspraxia 22, 27

early readers 48
Education Act 2, 3
educational needs 13
  principles 11

psychologist 15
emotional problems
  clumsy children and 99
  hyperactive children and
    105
  mathematics and 138-40
  speech and 37-8
encoding 15, 17
environment
  reading and 47, 58
epileptic 6
epistemic writing 74
ESN 6, 22
eye-movements 58

facial perception 18, 149
failure 12
figure-ground perception 56
fine motor skills 95, 99
  remediation 100
fluency 24, 37
  conditioning and 38-9
framework
  children's problems and
    15
functions 18
  secondary 18
  tertiary 18

Gerstmann's syndrome 45,50,
  55, 125, 144
grammar 75, 79
grapheme-phoneme correspondence 48, 55, 63-6,

graphophonic cues 66-8
gross movements 82, 96
  remediation 99

handedness 96
handicap 5
handwriting 83-6
  clumsy children and 97
  cursive 83
  manuscript 83
  paper and 84
  remediation 82-4
  visuo-motor problems 81
hearing loss 24
hemispherical dominance 46
  functioning 17